American Men of
Olympic Track and Field

American Men of Olympic Track and Field

Interviews with Athletes and Coaches

DON HOLST *and*
MARCIA POPP

McFarland & Company, Inc., Publishers
Jefferson, North Carolina, and London

LIBRARY OF CONGRESS ONLINE CATALOG DATA

Holst, Donald.
    American men of Olympic track and field : interviews with athletes and coaches / Don Holst and Marcia Popp.
        p.   cm.
    Includes index.

    ISBN 0-7864-1930-X (softcover : 50# alkaline paper)

    1. Track and field athletes—United States—Interviews.
    2. Track and field coaches—United States—Interviews.
    3. Olympics. I. Title.
    GV697.A1 H617   2005
    796.42'092—dc22   2004027685

British Library cataloguing data are available

On the cover: Glenn Cunningham (courtesy Mr. Cunningham and the University of Kansas Athletic Department)

Manufactured in the United States of America

McFarland & Company, Inc., Publishers
  Box 611, Jefferson, North Carolina 28640
    www.mcfarlandpub.com

When the Persian military officer Tigranes heard that the prize was not money but a crown [of olive], he could not hold his peace, but cried, "Good heavens, Mardonius, what kind of men are these that you have pitted us against? It is not for money they contend but for glory of achievement!"

Herodotus, *Histories*, 8.26.3

Table of Contents

Preface

by Don Holst (Interviewer)

Although athletes are frequently made to look like heroes, this book profiles athletes who truly *are* heroes—men whose lives, both on and off the field, reveal courage, persistence and decency. Although the numbers and statistics associated with these athletes are important because they identify their accomplishments in the world of sport, they are nonetheless secondary to the athletes' personal stories of triumph and defeat.

Among the men profiled in this book are those who went on to become authors, teachers, coaches, radio and television sports commentators, consultants, congressmen, actors, businessmen, military officers, social workers and ministers. Many continued competition in sports and remained physically fit long after their days as Olympians

These are men who would have achieved prominence and made significant contributions to society without having participated in the world's greatest games. Without exception, they exemplify the best in what is often referred to as "life after sport."

During our interviews, each retired athlete was presented with a series of questions designed to explore the influences in his life that helped him develop a unique set of values. They were asked to remember when they first knew there was such a thing as sport, and to describe some of the activities they participated in as children. They were also asked to recall any parental involvement and coaches who were particularly helpful.

What was the importance of academics in their formative years, and which extracurricular activities drew their interest? They were encouraged to talk about their friends in athletics and to describe how sports in general had influenced their lives. Because so much has changed since the time of their competition, I asked them to comment on the problems faced by athletes today—particularly the problems of professionalism and drugs.

Many had strong opinions about the amateurism that controlled athletic participation when they were competitors, and several had suggestions for improving the conduct of the Olympic Games.

Many of the athletes were surprised that there would be an interest in either their achievements or what they might have to say about the competitions of the present day. Yet the values and performances of these men stand as a reminder of a time when men participated in sport for the pure joy of it, and their fiercest efforts were for their own personal best.

All the interviews in this book are with male athletes and coaches. This indicates nothing more than the fact that my experience in track and field was limited to coaching men, and I felt I was best suited to interview and interpret the experiences of men in sport. The fine women track and field athletes I have known, including Helen Stephens (1936 Berlin Games 100 meter gold medalist), a close friend, have my deepest respect and admiration for their outstanding achievements and unfailing courage, both on and off the field. I must leave it to other writers, however, to chronicle the considerable accomplishments of these extraordinary women.

A Personal Note

My love of track and field began at the age of 12 when I participated in my first grade school track meet. I received three blue ribbons from Miss Nordling, a young teacher who did not stand on the steps in high heels at recess. Rather, she was always "chosen first" for games. That dear teacher cut out the ribbons from construction paper and wrote on them with white ink. In my lifetime, there have never been awards that meant more to me.

I learned the transient nature of winning and losing at an early age. The following year, a skinny red-haired kid moved to town from Colorado. He beat me in every event and even won my girlfriend!

Marcia Popp and I have paralleled the track world in the work we've done putting this book of interviews together. She would be a marathoner—good for the long run, patient, and always thinking of the best way to reach the goal. I would be the sprinter—out of the blocks and on my way, hoping to stay within the lane.

Preface

by Marcia Popp (Editor and Researcher)

In 1986, Dr. Don Holst, then professor of physical education at McKendree College, obtained a sabbatical leave to interview retired Olympic athletes. His goal was to preserve the reflections of a group of men who shared a common core of values—standards that motivated them and clearly reflected the ideals of the Olympic Games. Male track and field athletes were selected for this project because Dr. Holst's own coaching background was exclusively with men, and he felt he could best understand and communicate the relationships between male athletes and coaches.

At that time, I was chair of the Division of Education and Physical Education at McKendree, and I was very interested in the project Don proposed. During his sabbatical Don wrote letters, made phone calls, and crisscrossed the country to interview these men. Everywhere he visited, he was received graciously. The retired athletes gave generously of their time, sharing memories of participation in sport, and ideas about the current scene.

Don's enthusiasm for this project was contagious. Following my own retirement from college teaching, I agreed to help with editing the interviews and researching the accomplishments of the sixteen track and field Olympians and two Olympic coaches.

It is a testimony to the athletes' modesty that this kind of research was necessary. Although fourteen had been elected to the National Track and Field Hall of Fame, five to the Olympic Hall of Fame, and all to the halls of fame of their colleges or universities, none of them spoke at length about their honors and accomplishments.

After their participation in track and field competition, all went on to distinguish themselves in careers that included education, coaching, the military, business, journalism and entertainment. These men shared their talents and status in charitable ways, and each left the field having set the standard for the next generation of competitors or coaches.

As much as possible, I tried to include a brief biography of other athletes or coaches who were mentioned in the interviews. Athletes included in this collection who were mentioned by other interviewees are noted in bold type. A list of the athletes by their date of birth can be found in Appendix A. Appendix B provides brief descriptions of the events in which the Olympians competed. Appendix C lists the dtes and locations of the Modern Olympic Games.

I have been honored to meet only one of the athletes in person, although I have had several pleasant telephone conversations with the two Olympic coaches. All of the other men I know only through extensive research about their lives and the tapes Don created during the interviews. In the process, I have come to respect and admire them all.

From Abel Kiviat, who was born in 1892, to athletes who continue to serve their communities and compete in the Masters circuit today, the lives of these men touch three centuries. It has been my honor to help tell the stories of these exceptional 20th century athletes to readers in the 21st.

1

Lee Quency Calhoun

HIGH HURDLES • GOLD MEDAL
Born February 23, 1933, Laurel, Mississippi
Died June 22, 1989

Lee Calhoun was the first athlete to win Olympic gold medals in the 110-meter hurdles at two successive Olympic Games—in 1956 at Melbourne, Australia, and 1960 in Rome, Italy—both by the slimmest of margins (0.03 seconds and 0.01 second). In 1956, Calhoun won the Olympic high hurdles with a record 13.5.

Representing North Carolina Central College at Durham, Calhoun won the NCAA championship in the 110-meter hurdles in 1956 and 1957. He won the U.S. National Indoors Championship in the 110-meter hurdles in 1956, 1957 and 1959, and was the U.S. National Indoors Champion in the 60-yard hurdles in 1956 and 1957.

Career Achievements

- Before the 1956 Olympic Games, Calhoun's personal best in the 110-meter hurdles was 14.4 seconds. His time of 13.5 and a shoulder lunge at the finish line won Calhoun the gold. He'd picked up the lunge tactic from Jack Davis, who came in second.

- Although both men broke the Olympic record, Calhoun finished 0.03 seconds ahead of Davis.

- Just before the 1960 Olympics, Calhoun tied Martin Lauer's world record of 13.2 seconds for the 110-meter hurdles.

- In 1960, Calhoun and fellow U.S. teammate Willie May were

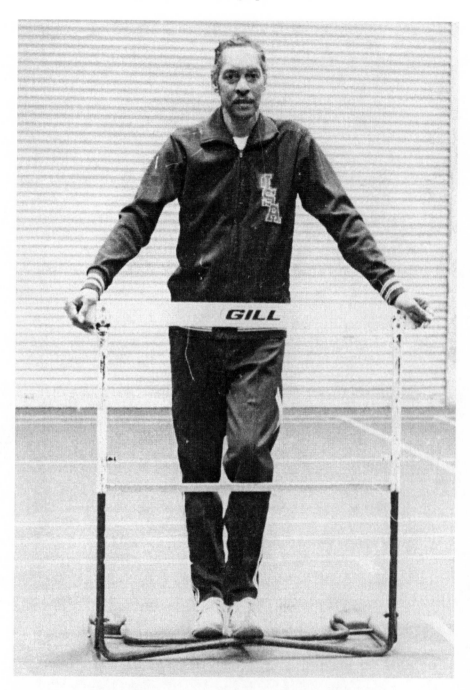

Lee Calhoun (high hurdles). (Courtesy Lee Calhoun.)

officially clocked at 13.8 seconds in the 110 meter hurdles, but the automatic timer gave Calhoun the victory by 0.01 second.

• Calhoun was inducted into the U.S. Track and Field Hall of Fame in 1974.

• He was inducted into the Olympic Hall of Fame in 1991.

• The Lee Calhoun High School Track and Field Invitational has been held at North Carolina Central University every year since 1993. It honors NCCU's first Olympic gold medalist.

• Western Illinois University at Macomb, Illinois, where Calhoun was head track coach, has hosted the Lee Calhoun Memorial Track Meet every spring since 1990.

Interview

"I knew there was only one way I could beat Jack. I had to get out of the blocks first, and lead him."

Interviewer's Notes

I first met Lee at the 1968 Olympics Training Center at South Lake Tahoe. At that time he was assistant track coach at Yale, and was a great help to our hurdlers at the camp. He was very well liked and a champion storyteller. It was obvious that his boyhood friends and growing up in rural Mississippi were as important to him as any of his records and gold medals.

Some 20 years later, I interviewed Lee at Western Illinois University where he was the head track coach. He generously shared information about his early life and the experiences that eventually brought him fame as a hurdler. In years and in spirit, he had remained a young man.

* * * * *

"I was born right after the Depression in Laurel, Mississippi," Calhoun begins, "along with Ralph Boston and Leontyne Price."

(Ralph Boston, long-jump world record holder, broke Jesse Owens' 25-year-old record in 1960, won the gold at the Olympics that same year, and went on to win the silver in '64 and bronze in '68. Leontyne Price was the first African-American to sing a major role at the La Scala Opera House, and the only opera singer to be represented in the list of "Remarkable American Women: 1776–1976" in *Life Magazine's* bicentennial issue in 1976.)

"Whites and blacks at that time were not very cordial to each other," Calhoun continues. "Sometimes we might be able to thumb a ride in a pickup truck or we just walked the entire distance. We would run, skip and joke around to make the trip shorter. It was also a way of developing stamina and strength. We paid little attention to the distance.

"Most of my time was spent on a farm," he says. "There are many chores you do there that help you become an athlete. We chased pigs and put them back in the pens, or ran after a chicken that Grandmother wanted for dinner. We walked behind a mule in the field and picked cotton. All these things helped develop the black kid. He was a laborer, even on his own piece of property or if he was share cropping.

"The black kids were not the muscular-type of individuals," Calhoun says. "What muscles they did have were strong. I can remember jumping over barbwire fences, and I still have a scar on my left leg because I stepped in a hole just before I took off. You got used to jumping across ditches, climbing trees, and night hunting for certain animals—in general just chasing things."

Calhoun remembers that one of the greatest things that happened to him was when he was seven years old and just learning how to run. "On Sunday, we went to church all day," he said, "first in the morning and then in the evening. The kids would all tag along, and I'd take the long way home because I wanted to be with my friends a little bit longer than just being at church. Some nights it would be stormy. If you have ever been in the country on a dark night and the moon and stars are not shining—it's dark!

"When you get a little lightning, you begin to see shadows. And I didn't care which way I went, there was always a cemetery between where I was and where I was going! The route I usually took going home was right by a real old cemetery. I used to think about a lot of things on the way home. The lightning would be playing and I would tell myself, 'Tonight I'm going to be brave and just walk.'

"So, I'd be walking along and there'd be a rustle in the grass. Down the road a little further I might hear something else back in the woods. All of a sudden there would be a big clap of thunder and that's when all my nerves were shot. I'd just take off and start running. Running two or three miles in those days was kids' play. I had no idea that this was leading me towards something better in my life.

"After we moved to Indiana we used to have what we called a block group. We lived at 21st and Jefferson in Gary, and there were these other groups that lived at 23rd and Madison, and 21st and Adams. We got along better with the Adams group than with the Madisons. Sometimes there would be a little fisticuffs and all-out battles, but no weapons were ever used," Calhoun says.

In his childhood, he played a game that involved a real-life long jump. "We used to play games within our own block," he remembers. "Our particular game involved one of the stupidest things I ever did as a kid. We had this thing where we would try to go from one end of the block to the other without touching the ground—by rooftop. We finally got up enough nerve to go about three fourths of a block—until we came to this flat top garage about 18 feet away. The garages were about that same width, so there wasn't much running space. Everyone always stopped there.

"To this day, I don't remember anybody else in my group ever making that leap. I tried it, after a long time of getting up my nerve. As I took off from this one garage, a board broke under my foot. I remember landing against the wall of the other garage, and it seemed as if it took me half an hour to slide to the ground. That ended that particular adventure.

"At that time Gary, Indiana, was just a bunch of sand," Calhoun says. "We would drive in stakes with nails in them and practice high jumping. There was some construction in the area and we would set up sawhorses and pretend they were hurdles.

"'Drop Hands and Run' was another game that we played. One guy out of the group would be chosen as 'It.' It was supposed to catch everyone else, with the help of the next person who was caught. We might play this game for three or four hours. The slower people were usually caught first.

"It was a strange kind of community where the athletes did not participate in athletics, though they were often better than the guys on the organized teams. We had guys who were sprinters who could outrun the guys who were on the high school team. The same thing was true about long distance runners. Athletics was not part of their real life, as it was ours," Calhoun says. "In school, our classes were pitted against each other for seasonal sports. I never attended a track meet and seldom a basketball game," he says.

"But I was the kind of kid that gave everything his all. In high school (Roosevelt High in Gary, Indiana) I joined the band and played my trumpet at the football games," he says. "I decided to go out for football that fall, but quickly found out that it was not my game. I weighed less than 130 pounds and stood about 5'10". They made me fourth string defensive end. I figured there was something better in sports than football.

"When track season rolled around, I decided to go out because it wasn't a contact sport and maybe I could do something. I knew I could high jump, and was already jumping about 5'10" or 5'11". So, as a 17-year-old junior in 1950, I started my track career."

Remembering his coach, Calhoun says, "The coach would stand there with a great big paddle, slapping it on his leg while he talked to us. He looked us straight in the eye and sent the message that either we did it or we didn't. Although I just missed going to State my first year, it gave me a sense of growth.

"The following year I read about Harrison Dillard and Milt Campbell and some of the others who were doing well in high school and college. I started looking at my opponents in the immediate area and figured that if they could do it, so could I. I started off again as a high jumper.

"At the first outdoor meet my high school coach called me over and said, 'Lee, I need you in the hurdles today. Turner Hunter, our best hurdler isn't here.'

"I left my high jump area and entered the hurdles. I took second behind the state champion. I also won over the other two hurdlers from my school. Then I went back and won the high jump."

"Monday at practice the coach came over and asked, 'Are you ready?' My reply was, 'Ready for what?'

"'For your challenge,' he said. 'The three guys in the hurdles want to challenge you.'

"I really didn't want to run the hurdles and told the coach they could have their positions. He told me that wasn't the way they did things. I had to give them the opportunity to win back the positions they had lost. Since Turner wasn't there, they had the right to see if I was better than him.

"We passed this thing back and forth for about five minutes," Calhoun remembers. "All the time we were talking, my blood pressure was beginning to build. Now, if I had been smart, I would have lost the race. But the race went off three times, and I won each time by a greater margin. As a result, I got stuck with the hurdles.

"When they found I could run the high hurdles, they automatically thought I could run the low hurdles. In my senior year I made it to State in both the high jump and the high hurdles. The day of the meet, it was one of those times in Indiana when the weather decides it will show you it can do anything at any time it feels like it." Calhoun remembers that it rained, snowed, sleeted and hailed—a little bit of everything.

"I was favored to take second in the high jump and second in the hurdles," he says. "I hit the first five hurdles and scored one point for the team. Luckily, we still won the state championship.

"After graduation, I went to work in the steel mill, as all good industrial-city boys did in those days. I was not offered any scholarships, even though I lived in the heart of the Big Ten. It didn't make me feel any less of a man at that particular time," Calhoun says. "I still didn't understand what athletics was all about. I just did it for the fun of it.

"Coach LeRoy Walker, from North Carolina, was in the stands at the state meet. He was looking at someone else, not particularly me. But he just had a hunch, he told me, about my attitude about things, and was taking a shot at recruiting me. I kept refusing his offers to go to college."

Dr. LeRoy T. Walker, legendary collegiate track and field coach, was elected to the U.S. Track and Field Hall of Fame and the Olympic Hall of Fame. He was president of the U.S. Olympic Committee, and in 1976 was the first African-American to serve as the head coach for the U.S. men's track and field team.

Calhoun continues that "about the same time, the young lady in my life made a wrong turn and married someone else. That kind of cleared my mind about leaving town and getting away from the vicinity where she would be living. I finally accepted LeRoy Walker's invitation to attend North Carolina Central University. I spent two years there and won the conference both years.

"I was amazed by Coach Walker's recruiting. Despite all the problems I had at the state high school meet, he was going to make a hurdler out of me in college, where the hurdles are 3 inches higher.

"In those days a lot of the hurdles weren't built like they are now. You hit one and it was like hitting a wall," he remembers. "Those old hurdles might have been what developed me into a technical hurdler. I never had the blazing speed that most of the hurdlers possess. The first six months that I worked in the college highs," Calhoun remembers, "there were tears in my eyes about every day. I had bruises on me everywhere.

"Dr. Walker trained us with the overload repetition method. I was in such good condition that at the Penn Relays, for example, I ran the 4 × 100, 4 × 200, sprint medley, the high hurdles *and* the mile relay."

Just before Calhoun went into the Army during the Korean War, he ran a meet at Madison Square Garden, where he finished third behind Harrison Dillard. "I was really pleased with that particular race," Calhoun says. "Then I just sort of disappeared for two years.

"I was lucky in Korea, as my duty station was a hospital. The reason I got stationed at the hospital was because I knew how to run a movie projector! We were located eight miles from Seoul. If you wanted to go to town you had to catch a bus or one of our trucks. I asked one of the coaches in special services if there was a track team and he told me there wasn't any interest. I got a list of all the units in Korea and mailed a letter of information.

"It was amazing the people you could find in the little cracks and corners," Calhoun says. "Sherman Willer, who was in the '52 Games; Aleck Hickman, a 9.5 sprinter; Ansel Robinson, a premiere hurdler from Fresno State; Willie Attebury, a Michigan hurdler. We kept finding these kinds of people. Our second year we teamed with the Air Force and ran against the Japanese National Team in Tokyo and won. It was a real surprise to the Japanese that our military team was that strong."

Asked about the problem with drugs in sports, Calhoun says, "Drugs never seemed to be a consideration of the track athlete until 1960–64. Athletes started paying attention to what others were taking to enhance their performances, particularly steroids. I believe that with the controls now in place, an athlete is foolish to even consider doing drugs, because they know they are going to be tested. And if they are caught they will be banned.

"More important is the terrible things it does to your body. You really cheat yourself by not knowing what you really can do as an individual, without the extra help.

"I believe we are on the upside of the drug problem, however," Calhoun says. "Individuals are experimenting more, but we punish our athletes for taking drugs. In some countries they are rewarded for their performances. We are trying to tell our athletes to stop taking drugs because it is going to harm them. Other countries are researching how they can manage non-detection of drugs. Either you get with people who are making the drugs or you do it on your own and get caught.

"Several years ago, prior to the 1984 Olympics in Los Angeles, a person came out with a statement, 'I could give a person anabolic steroids and have them monitored, so it would never be detected.' This is an idea of what is happening today. Perhaps they are given something else, which will mask the drug. There seems to be as much research into the masking of drugs as in the production.

"After college and with my military service taken care of, I moved back to Gary, Indiana. At that time, I was 25 years old. It was a very difficult situation, because the closest indoor athletic facility was at the University of Chicago thirty miles away. Willie May, who was second to me in the '60 Olympics, was doing his student teaching from Indiana University at the high school where I graduated."

May was a three-event state champion from Blue Island High School in 1955, and was the Olympic silver medalist in the high hurdles in the 1960 Rome Olympics. Later, he became a track coach, athletic director, and member of the track advisory committee of the Illinois High School Association.

"I worked as a city administrator at that time," Calhoun says. "Willie and I would jump in a car and work out for a couple hours, then drive back. People thought we were crazy. Well, maybe we were. There was no other alternative, unless you wanted to work in one of the hallways at a high school. I think the degree of difficulty was the thing that pulled most of us through. This is what most athletes look at—where you are going to live and train.

"Harrison Dillard once told me the only place he had to work out was the YMCA. I lived in Cleveland for a year, and I went to that same YMCA and saw what he was talking about. There was a running track on the balcony—a three-lane, banked affair. Running on that constant turn was bad for your ankles. You could do short sprint work on the basketball court. He told me the biggest part of his workout was standing against the wall while running as hard as he could, pushing against the wall."

In 1958, Calhoun was suspended from amateur competition because he accepted gifts for appearing on the television game show *Bride and Groom*. His amateur standing was reinstated a year later. He continued, "I took a year's leave while the AAU decided about the gifts I received on a television game show. I trained that year the way Harrison did. Once you have laid the foundation and stay in condition, you can be anywhere. I've passed this on to my athletes at every school I've worked. If you can't go outside, go to your basement or your living room. Do situps, calisthenics, run in place, and stay in shape. Don't just look out the window and say it's ten degrees. You can't do the technical things, but you can keep in sound physical condition.

"Jack Davis was the heir-apparent to Harrison Dillard's gold medal. I was in position to beat both of them. Milt Campbell was one of the good hurdlers but favored the decathlon. Elias Gilbert from Winston-Salem—you can name them, we had 'em in those days. Any one of them could win a race.

"I had gone undefeated in seven big time meets and I guess Jack Davis was kind of bitter, because he thought he should be winning. He made a statement, which one of my friends passed on to me, that I was a 'flash in the pan' and a good indoor hurdler, but wouldn't be able to go the distance outdoors.

"That kind of got me thinking and it also made me angry," Calhoun says. "Somewhere during the outdoor season I was going to beat Jack Davis. We had our first competition at the Marine Corps meet in Quantico,

Virginia. Jack had been training on the West Coast and I'd trained on the East. There is a lot of difference between those places. He beat me with a time of 13.7. My time was 13.8. What he didn't know was that I was really happy about that 13.8. I didn't care about losing; it was the first time I had ever broken 14.0 in competition!

"Then he went back and made a few more statements. I said, 'Good, that will just put more fuel on the fire.' I kept running on the East Coast and I finally got down to 13.7. If you take an East Coast athlete and transplant him to the West, you would think he was raised there. This is what happened to me that year. It was an Olympic year, so I took all my college finals early. Then the high jumper and I moved out West.

Jack Davis equaled the world's record at the National AAU Trials. In the finals he was next to Harrison. Somehow he got tangled up with Harrison's spikes, and I went on to win the race—the first time I had defeated Jack.

"The next week was the Olympic Trials. We were to be eliminated until there were eight of us left, including Jack Davis, Joel Shankle, Milt Campbell, Harrison Dillard, Elias Gilbert, and me. The gun went off and Jack and I were stride for stride for ten hurdles. We finished in a dead heat, and Joel Shankle was third.

"Joel went to Duke University when I was at North Carolina Central, which was across town. We used to work out at 9 P.M. Joel, Dave Sime, a couple of my friends, and I would have some good runs on their long straightway. That Dave Sime was quite a runner. He showed up with his baseball uniform and spikes and asked to be timed in the 100. He ran a 9.5.

Sime, who was also an excellent baseball player, held world records in the 100-yards, the 220 and 200-meter races, and the 220-yard low hurdles. When he was 36 years old, he ran 9.6 for the 100 yards. Joel Shankle won the bronze at the '56 Olympics, was the 1955 NCAA long jump champion, four-time Penn Relays champion, two-time All American and seven time ACC champion.

"The Olympics were held in late fall because of Australia being in a different hemisphere. We trained at Pomona College, but I started getting stale and dropped out of competition for a couple of weeks," Calhoun says.

"When I really started putting my mind back into training, we were in Australia and Jack beat me in every warm-up race. On a football field, he set a new world's record. I was second, Milt Campbell third, and Joel Shankle fourth. This win got Jack's confidence up again.

"The same thing happened in the sprints. Leamon King, who had a bad day at the trials, beat Bobby Morrow, Thane Baker, and Ira Murchison every time they ran in the warm-up meets.

"I have always believed a coach's position on a National Team is more that of a supervisor than a coach. He knows nothing about the individual athlete. What got the athlete to the Olympics was not the National Coach. I was being pressured into some situations that I didn't like, so I asked them to just shoot the gun and run the watch.

"I finally moved across town in Melbourne and worked out pretty much by myself. There was an old Australian over at my site and every day he showed up with a stopwatch. It was now about a week prior to our races in the Games. I didn't have a stopwatch, so I asked him if he would time me in the hurdles at 120 yards.

"I wanted to run three times, five minutes apart. He asked me what I wanted for time and I told him 14.2. He told me I couldn't do it.

"I said, 'Maybe not, but I want to find out.' So I ran 14.2 on all three sets. He told me he was betting on me.

"The day of the races, everything was smooth through the prelims and semifinals. I knew there was only one way I could beat Jack. I had to get out of the blocks first, and lead him. I couldn't catch him from behind because he was too strong. I wanted him to come after me, and if he made any kind of mistake, I was gone."

"When the gun went off, I was wired for sound and part of the projection that came out of that gun! I was *gone*! I led Jack through several hurdles and he caught me at eight. We ran nip and tuck across nine and through the finish line, where I edged him out by a nudge of my shoulder. That was when we both ran 13.5 for a new Olympic and World's record." The U.S. team took 1, 2, and 3.

"At the next Games I had some ups and downs, including the one-year ban by the AAU. In 1960, I lost every indoor race to Hayes Jones, but I was determined to beat him in the Garden. I ran so hard and fast trying to catch him, I couldn't raise my leg on the last hurdle. I caught my spikes on the top of the hurdle and it pitched me across the finish line in second place. I hit that wooden track and it took three layers of skin off my shoulder and elbow.

"I lost the National AAU Championships to Hayes Jones, but I rounded out in shape just in time. We ran at Stanford for the trials. Most everybody else lived at Stanford; I lived in Berkeley with Vance Robinson, Josh Culbraith, and Art Briggs from Jamaica.

"When the day came for the finals, I was a little nervous. The official wanted to nail my blocks in. I gave him a piece of my mind and let him know that no one touched my blocks prior to a race. It was the first time in my career that I ever said anything bad to an official. We ran 13.4 that day, which equaled the World's Record.

"In the Rome games," Calhoun remembers, "the track wasn't good for me, because it rained right before our competition. I'll never forget—they were reading the wind gauge, and we had always had the wind behind us. When I came out of the blocks against Willie May and crashed the first hurdle, I thought I was out of it.

"I kept fighting back and I finally caught up with him. We went over the last hurdle pretty even and about halfway to the tape, I think he kind of glanced over at me. That gave me all I needed to go for the tape. I dove for it, broke the tape with the top of my head, and was leaning so far forward I couldn't get up.

"He teased me for a long time, but actually he was serious. He used to come to my house every day and say, 'Let me see my medal.' Years later, a television station had a different angle shot of the finish line. He finally agreed that I had won the race.

"I would like to have run against Dick Attlesey from Southern Cal, but he got hurt with a torn gluteus muscle. He was so tall (6'4") that he had to shuffle between the hurdles. The speed was there and I always wondered what he would have done if he'd had a chance to mature in the high hurdles.

"If I had to do it over again, I might have done some work with the weights. In my training, I only used them one year. They were homemade affairs, you know, a couple gallon cans of cement on the ends of a pipe. I did a few curls, but that was about it. It was a poor black school and there wasn't much money. Coach Walker never mentioned weights.

"Dan Ferris and Pincus Sober were running the Games and had modeled themselves in some ways after Avery Brundage." All three men championed amateurism. Daniel Ferris was a sprinter who joined the Amateur Athletic Union in 1907. He was personal secretary to James Sullivan, and took Sullivan's place as secretary-treasurer of the AAU in 1914, where he served for 43 years. Pincus "Pinky" Sober was chairman of the International Amateur Federation Technical Committee, and a track announcer at Madison Square Garden.

Avery Brundage was a three-time National AAU champion in the all around and pentathlon and represented the U.S. in the 1912 Olympic Games. A multi-millionaire contractor, he served as president of the National AAU (seven terms), the U.S. Olympic Committee (1929–1953), and the International Olympic Committee (1952–1972).

"Personally," Calhoun says, "I believe he was the wrong person to emulate. Avery's past history proved that he was only in favor of what the athlete could do for the reputation of the United States. He, being a millionaire, thought everyone should make sacrifices. His sacrifice was living in a hundred-dollar room; my sacrifice was living in an eight-dollar room. There is a marked difference.

"I think this got the athletes into trouble by trying to get as much as they could. The only thing I resent is that I had a good offer by NBC to sue the AAU on my behalf. In the case of **Wes Santee**, they could have slapped his wrist, but they banned him for life. I was also banned for life.

"The only thing that saved me was that I was working for the Chairperson of the Lake Erie Association. At the time, the AAU was buying a house on Fifth Avenue in New York, and the Association was supposed to raise so much money for the house.

"The man I was working for had raised his share, a ballpark figure of about $35,000. He would not give them the money at the convention until they disposed of my case. They had a National roll call vote on the floor, and gave me a year's suspension from the date of infraction.

"The suspension I received was for getting married on a National Television Program called *Bride and Groom*. Everybody and his brother were getting married on the program because of the gifts they received. There was nothing illegal that I could see, except that the AAU said I was capitalizing on my national fame.

"The AAU had never contacted me, but I heard through the grapevine in New York that I would be suspended if I went on the program. A reporter from Indianapolis called me and wanted to know if I'd read the papers. I didn't know what he was talking about. He told me the AAU was threatening to do all kinds of things to me. I went by to see Dan Ferris and Pincus Soper, and we had an hour's discussion about just why I was being singled out for this particular punishment.

"I asked them, 'Suppose I got married in a cornfield. If you are married any place other than on television and received gifts, there would be no punishment.' I asked them about the tennis player who won $13,000 on *Name that Tune*—What was the National Tennis Federation going to do about that? He was an amateur and I was an amateur.

"I guess the difference between competing in those days and now is, if you don't represent a university, you can do about what you want. Renaldo Nehemiah from Maryland got angry about being run too much, and quit the university team. But he maintained his student status. You can do about anything you want to now, as long as you don't represent a university."

"I believe the Athletic Congress is increasingly coming to the aid of the athlete. We used to get $15 per day to live in California, or New York

City. If you didn't room with someone or stay in a real cheap hotel and eat a bare minimum of meals, you couldn't make it.

"In football and basketball, the athlete gets a check every month. In track and field, the athletes come from everywhere and may not be associated with anyone. Look at Merriweather—he was watching television one day and said, 'I can run that fast.' He put away his doctor's uniform, put on swimming trunks, went down to the track and blew them away. If you can run, jump or throw, you don't need the backing.

"I have always been a fairly quiet person and have not gone out to make a lot of friends. I've never had any problem with the foreign athletes. Martin Lauer and I are friends. The two of us held the world's record in the high hurdles for a number of years.

"I believe that athletes around the world today are much closer, and get along better with people from other countries, because they see each other more often. When I was competing, every two years I might meet a Russian. We got to know them better at the Olympics because they could not be controlled by their government; they were at dances and in the cafeteria.

If the concept is fostered of having one Olympic site in Greece where all athletes go to train and participate, without politics, many problems would be solved. I have been praying for this to happen."

In later life, Calhoun was a college track coach at Grambling University, Yale University, and Western Illinois University. He was also an assistant coach for the track and field team at the 1976 Olympics.

Brenda Calhoun-Cash, his daughter, was ranked in the top 12 nationally in the 100 meter dash and the 100 meter hurdles from 1976 to 1981. She was an Olympic trials semifinalist in the 1976 Olympic trials. At Arizona State University, Cash was All American for four years. She set school records in the 100 meter dash and 100 meter hurdles, and was a member of the 4 × 100 meter relay team that set a national record.

2

Glenn Cunningham

MIDDLE DISTANCES • SILVER MEDAL
IN THE 1500 METERS
Born August 4, 1909, Elkhart, Kansas
Died March 10, 1988, Menifee, Arkansas

Glenn Cunningham, considered in his day to be the fastest human being alive, earned credentials for fame, both on and off the athletic field. He was undoubtedly the best middle-distance runner of the 1930s, and was almost certainly one of the most enduringly popular track athletes of his time.

Admired for his courage and good sportsmanship, Cunningham's achievements included 13 Big Six Conference Championships, two NCAA titles in the mile, nine AAU Championships, multiple world records, and an Olympic silver medal. Cunningham won the Sullivan Award in 1933 as the nation's top amateur athlete. That year, he won the NCAA mile, the AAU 800-meter run and 1500-meter run. He set a world record of 4:06.7 for the mile in the Princeton Invitational Meet.

Among the nicknames given to Cunningham during his athletic career were: The Elkhart Express, The Kansas Flyer, The Kansas Iron Man, The Fastest Man Alive, World's Fastest Miler, and World's Fastest Human Being.

Career Achievements

- In 1930, Cunningham was the greatest scholastic miler in history. During his senior year in high school, he set a new state record of 4:28.3 for the mile. In July of that year, he posted a new national record of 4:24.7 at the National Interscholastic Meet in Chicago.

- The Big Six Conference named Cunningham the outstanding runner of the 1931 cross-country season.

- Cunningham was undefeated in the half-mile, mile, and two-mile races in the 1932 conference schedule. He was the first runner in conference history to win the half-mile and mile runs in the Big Six Championships.

- He won the NCAA 1500-meter run championship in 1932, and was the first NCAA track champion from Kansas to win the mile run at the National Intercollegiate Meet.

- Cunningham qualified for the Olympic team that same year, and finished fourth in the 1500-meter run at the Los Angeles Games.

- During his years at the University of Kansas, Cunningham won two National Collegiate titles and eight AAU championships.

- In the spring of 1934, Cunningham set a new indoor record of 3:52.3 for the 1500-meter run. In the Columbian Mile the following month, he ran a 4:08.4 mile, a new indoor world record.

- In June of that same year, Cunningham defeated Princeton's star miler by forty yards and established a new world record of 4:06.7. At this time he had completed seven of the thirteen fastest miles ever run by a human being.

- In the spring of 1935, Cunningham broke the world record for the 1000-yard run. At the AAU championships that year, he broke his own indoor record for the 1500-meter run by almost two seconds.

- Cunningham was the AAU 1500-meter champion from 1935 through 1938.

- In a two-week period in 1934, Cunningham set an 800-meter world record of 1:49.7, and a one mile record of 4:06.8 that stood for three years.

- Cunningham ran an indoor one mile of 4:04.4 in 1938 at Dartmouth, paced by four Dartmouth runners. This was well below the world record for that time. However, because four quarter milers had set the pace for him, the International Amateur Athletic Federation refused to accept his time as an official record.

Glenn Cunningham (middle distances) rounds the curve. (Courtesy Glenn Cunningham and the University of Kansas Athletic Department.)

Had it been recognized, the run would have held the record until 1955.

- In 1933, Cunningham received the Helms World Trophy, an award given to outstanding athletes from all continents. (Other prominent U.S. winners of the Helms Trophy have included: Avery Brundage [AAU, 1918]; Johnny Weissmuller of "Tarzan" fame [1923]; Jesse Owens [1935]; **Bob Mathias** [1948]; **Wes Santee** [1954]; **Al Oerter** [1964]; and **Bill Toomey** [1969].)

- Cunningham was in the first class (1974) of inductees into the National Hall of Fame established by the Athletics Congress (later the Track and Field Hall of Fame). He was also inducted into the Elkhart Sports Hall of Fame, the Kansas State High School Athletic Association Hall of Fame, and the University of Kansas Athletic Hall of Fame.

- He was voted the Millrose Games Outstanding Performer in 1933, finishing second in 1934 and 1935. (The Millrose Games are part of the U.S. Track and Field "Golden Spike" tour, and have been held at Madison Square Garden since 1914—the longest continuing event in the Garden's history.)

- In 2000, Cunningham was inducted posthumously into the Millrose Games Hall of Fame, along with four-time gold medal Olympian Carl Lewis (sprints, long jump, 4 × 100 relay) and 15-year world-ranked hurdles champion, Greg Foster.

Interview

"You never elevate yourself by beating someone else down."

Interviewer's Notes

A sportswriter was quoted as saying that what he and other writers liked about Cunningham was that "he was a great runner who didn't go around telling everyone that he was." During the fall of 1938, I was a school crossing guard at Lincoln School in Marysville, Kansas. While I was at my post on graveled U.S. 77, one of my friends came by and told me the world's fastest runner, Glenn Cunningham, was going to run at the high school. I couldn't get away to see him run. Fifty years later, when I called Conway, Arkansas, Mrs. Cunningham said, "You come on down;

we have plenty of room." I spent three days with the Cunninghams, enjoying their great hospitality.

The first question I asked Glenn was about the episode of tragedy and bravery that marked his early life. As so much had been written about the event, I wanted to hear from him exactly what happened.

* * * * *

"In 1916," Cunningham begins, "we lived on a farm two miles from the school. I was seven years old at the time; we walked to school in the morning and home at night.

"The young man who taught us wasn't very punctual," Cunningham remembers. "He was supposed to build a fire and get the building warm by the time the students arrived. This particular morning we got there first, so we were to start the fire."

Cunningham explained that the school was the social center of the community—the only place to hold meetings. There was no electricity, so for a meeting held the previous evening people had brought gasoline for their lanterns. Some of that gasoline found its way into the can of kerosene used for starting a fire in the mornings.

"My brother Floyd shook down the ashes and apparently didn't notice the live coals from the night before," Cunningham says. "Normally, the fire was dead in the morning, but the meeting from the night before had gone late, and some live coals had held over."

Floyd poured from what he thought was a five-gallon can of kerosene, and as he was pouring it the gasoline exploded.

"We ran out," Cunningham remembers, "and my brother told my sister to throw sand on us to put out the fire. But it was midwinter, and the ground was frozen." Cunningham said that the next thing they did was to start running home.

"My God," he says, "the burns were so bad, my brother was burned clear through his abdominal walls and on his back, clear through to his kidneys. Flesh was dropping off our legs—it had burned so deep.

"As we ran home, I guess there were still flames coming off our clothes, those that were left on us."

Cunningham remembers that Floyd's clothes were practically all burned off by the time he got out of the school. His sister took off her coat and put it on him.

"It was cold and the wind was blowing," Cunningham says. "We ran the two miles home, and when we got there my older sister took off Floyd's shoes and set them on a little wooden sled. The shoes and sled both burned up," he says.

"My parents weren't home when we got there," Cunningham remembers. "My grandmother was sick and staying on another farm, a couple of miles from our place. In those days, when you got sick, someone always 'sat up' with you. My other brother and sister had to run over and get my parents, and my brother and sister had already run the two miles with us before they started.

"When my brother and I were burned, there wasn't anything our neighbors wouldn't have done for us. How could we have paid those debts? I know what they did, and I will never forget it. We were all of humble backgrounds, just common ordinary people—all of us."

Because of the risk of infection that could take his life, the Cunninghams' doctor wanted to amputate Glenn's legs. But his parents persisted with every treatment they could find. His mother rubbed ointments into the burns and when they had healed enough, she massaged them and helped him bend his legs again.

"I knew that I would not only walk again," he says, "but that I would be able to run. My father had a saying 'Never quit. Work your problem out,' and that's what I did."

Months of recovery, infection and deliberation over the amputation of his severely damaged legs only seemed to strengthen his resolve to walk again. Of that time, he said: "It hurt like thunder to walk, but it didn't hurt at all when I ran. So for five or six years, about all I did was run."

Of his serious injuries, Cunningham told journalists: "To me it was a challenge. Once a person accepts something like that as a handicap, you're licked before you start." As a young adult and adult runner, Cunningham required at least an hour to prepare for a race because of the damage done to his legs in the childhood burn accident. Preparation included a massage of his legs to improve circulation, followed by a long warm-up period.

When asked about his introduction to sports, Cunningham says that he didn't know much about organized sports. "Our parents played a lot with us," he says. "We would go with our father out to work and it was always a matter of competition. When we went to the barn to do chores, he would divide up us kids, setting us at different distances from the barn. Then, after we were in our places, we would race to see who could get to the barn first. Whatever we were doing," Cunningham says, "picking maize or watermelons—it was always a matter of competition."

"I can remember an old pony I had. When I was about three years old, I would take a jug of water and ride out to the field, so my dad could have a cool drink. Our family was always working, but always happy. We had few material things, always a lot to eat, and we didn't know we were poor. We didn't need money to be wealthy," he says, with conviction. "We had good health and seldom got sick."

Cunningham remembers that when he ran his first competitive race, he weighed just a little over 70 pounds. "I still had on my winter underwear, along with a pair of overalls, a shirt, wool sweater and basketball shoes. I was twelve years old at the time. One of the rules was that you had to weigh 70 pounds to get into the older kids' race. The man that weighed me in said I just made it."

"The officials wanted me to run in another class with the smaller, younger kids," Cunningham says. "Well, I beat all the high school kids and won the race."

Because his parents saw little value in their children competing in athletics, Cunningham left immediately after the race. "I got thinking about that," he says, "so I jumped on my pony and went home. My plans were to pick up the medal on Monday morning."

Unfortunately, when he went to get his award, someone told him it had been lost. Cunningham later found out that the medal was given to the high school miler who came in second—a disappointment for the twelve-year-old boy who had really won the race. As an adult, Cunningham said, "I've run some big races—including the Olympics—but no race was more important than the one I ran at 12."

Cunningham remembers that there was no track team during his early years in Elkhart, Kansas. "We did, however, have meets where each class competed against the other," he says. "When we were freshmen, there were three of us who performed quite well. But the principal didn't want us to go to meets and the athletic coach wasn't interested in us either.

"One of our English teachers took us to our first meet and we won everything we entered. Our next meet was at Syracuse and they had a miler who had set the record the year before. On meet day, there was a lot of wind, as is common in Kansas. All my hard work on the farm, like scooping wheat at the grain elevator, really helped. I kept running around the track, and finally won!

"The announcer said: 'Cunningham has established a new world's record by 18.9 seconds!' I thought the coach would really be pleased with that. But you know what? He jumped down my throat and didn't allow me to run another mile race that year. He had told me to follow the other runners' pace until the last 200 yards.

"Later, I went to Chicago for the National Scholastic Meet, which was held at Stagg Field. I followed the coach's advice and ran hard toward the end of the race. As I was going across the field to see my coach, Alonzo

Stagg stopped me. Mr. Stagg said, 'Son, that was the greatest finish I have ever seen on a mile run, college or otherwise.'

"When I reached my coach, he asked me what the man had said, and if I knew who he was. When I told him, he said that was the greatest compliment I would ever get. The coach, however, still refused to let me set the pace during a race."

Cunningham had set the world record in the high school mile, and when he returned to Elkhart, people came from miles around for a big reception. "My parents and I rode down the street in a convertible," he says. "People threw paper confetti everywhere.

"It was my father's job to take care of the streets in Elkhart, so afterwards I got busy helping him sweep up. The editor of the paper yelled to me: 'Glenn Cunningham, what are you doing, sweeping up this mess? This was all made for you!'

"I told him that I was out there last week and the week before and I'd be out there next week, so what was the matter with today? Just because I went to Chicago and set a record, that didn't make any difference. I was the same person I was before and had the same job today.

"You know," Cunningham says, "it never occurred to me that anyone would ask that question. I always helped my father with whatever he did. He had been on that street job for quite a while and I always helped him."

Although Cunningham had set a new national high school record for the mile (4:24.7) during competition at the National Interscholastic Meet in Chicago in 1930, NCAA rules prohibited him from competing at the collegiate level until he was a sophomore.

When Cunningham went to college, most of the boys his age made money working in a drugstore. Cunningham says that he hauled ashes, cleaned out privies or did any hard labor he could do. This meant he could earn thirty dollars a day, in contrast to the lighter work that paid only a few dollars.

"I had to work my way through," he says. "My parents couldn't give me any money, but I tried to send them some when they needed it.

"In later years," he says, "I told my kids that I was as proud of the calluses on my hands as I was of the degrees I earned or the trophies I won. The education and awards haven't changed me any. I am the same person. Material things do not change my feelings or interest in people. I believe every individual has dignity and deserves a certain respect.

"When I was a senior in high school, a lot of coaches tried to convince me to go to their school," Cunningham says. "I went to California after I graduated, because the weather was warmer and my legs worked better. But the minute I landed there, I knew it wasn't for me.

"I came back home, and went up to the University of Kansas. I rode the train, and the first thing I did when I got off was to phone coach Brutus Hamilton to tell him I was in town. I told him I was interested in going to Kansas if I could get a job. This was during the Depression in the fall of 1930.

"Brutus and some of the other coaches came down and we visited. One of the first things he asked me was 'How fast do you run?'

"I asked him if he meant competitive or otherwise, and he answered, 'Well, both.'

"I told him my best time in a meet was 4:24.7, and in practice I had run under 4:00.0. Now these times were in high school, and I knew Coach Hamilton didn't believe it. He didn't say anything, but he must have thought, 'Yeah, were they timing you with a calendar?'

"During my running career, there were many athletes capable of breaking the four minute mile. The coaches set up that barrier—what I call the psychological barrier. I used to have coaches tell me that you couldn't run without a good transverse arch. I could take my toes and lay them back on top of my foot. I really didn't have feet to run on. The only thing I had was that big toe to drive off of.

"I've got these scars here on my legs where the flesh fell off, and they're now covered with scar tissue. I really didn't have any business running. I was supposed to be an invalid after those burns, because at that time there was little in the way of burn treatment. The doctors told my folks that my legs should be amputated, because if I got an infection I could lose my life. But it didn't happen, because I knew I would walk again and eventually run.

"In 1932, we were getting ready for the Olympics and Brutus Hamilton was our coach. (Hamilton, a decathlete, won the silver medal at the 1920 Games in Belgium. If he had finished the 1500-meter race six seconds faster, he would have won the gold.) We were training at the University of Kansas with Jim Bausch, Buster Charles and Clyde Coffman from the Indian Institute at Haskell. Jim Baush won the decathlon in that year. Venske set the record for the mile with a time of 4.10. Paavo Nurmi had run a 4:10.4 and that was thought to be the limit.

"It was at this time that Brutus came out with his 'statistical limits' of performance, and I believe he had the mile at 4:00.6. I told him that I thought he was wrong, because I had already done better myself. He never discussed it with me, because I think he just didn't believe it, and nobody else did either.

"A group of track enthusiasts came up to my hotel room, and one of their first questions was 'How fast will the mile eventually be run?' I told them it would go well under four minutes—probably 3:48.

"That came out in the paper the next day and Lawson Robinson, the coach at Pennsylvania and also the Olympic coach, wrote an article about this guy from the sticks predicting a mile under four minutes. He said that as one of the coaches who had worked with the best middle distance runners in the country for the past twenty years, he saw no possibility of a four minute mile."

Cunningham says that he told Coach Hamilton, "This is the reason we haven't had a sub-four minute mile. Coaches don't believe it can be done, so how are the boys to believe it, if you don't?

"Jim Ryun later ran under four minutes as a high school boy," he adds.

"During the 1932 Olympics, I entered the 1500 meters and finished fourth. By the time I was ready for the Berlin Olympics in 1936, I had been a World Record Holder, having run a 4:06.7 mile at the Princeton Invitational in 1934.

"I ran at Princeton in 1934," Cunningham says, "and set a new world's record. Just before the race started, I had finished my warm-up and was going for a rubdown when I stepped in a hole along the track. I popped that ankle and could hardly hobble into the dressing room.

"The trainer put a heavy, basket weave tape wrap on the ankle and I went out and set a new world's record. My ankle was swelling so fast," he remembers, "the tape ripped across the bottom of my foot.

"We got on an air-conditioned train to go to California, and I really wanted to get out of that race, because I could hardly walk. I was told, 'Just step on the track; you don't have to run.' I told them that if I was going to start, I'd finish it. I still could barely walk when I competed in the Nationals in Milwaukee.

"I never had a tough race when I was in shape," Cunningham says. "When I was out of shape, they were all tough! All the traveling hurt my performance, because you could hardly get a workout, except to skip rope a little and do a few calisthenics. Then it was a drive to the airport to fly where we were going to run—back to the car, and maybe another 500 miles, in a limited amount of time, for another race.

"There were many good runners from south and southwest Kansas," he says, "like Jimmy Ryun, **Wes Santee**, Billy Tidwell, Archie San Romani, and Thane Baker, who was from my hometown of Elkhart. There weren't a lot of people in that part of Kansas, but there sure were some good runners.

"Kids in these towns were really impressionable. They had me run down Main Street after the '36 Olympics, and Thane, who was just five or six at the time, saw me there in my Olympic uniform and decided he wanted to do that more than anything."

Baker grew up to become a four-time All-American sprinter at Kansas State University and two-time U.S. Olympian. He set or tied eight world or American records from 1952 to 1956 in distances of 60 to 300 yards. He won the silver at 200 meters in the 1952 Helsinki Olympic Games, and was a triple medal winner in the 1956 Olympics at Melbourne.

Cunningham says that his burns made it difficult for him to warm up properly for a race. "I experienced some of the worst weather when I was in Berlin for the 1936 Olympics," he says. "When we got to Germany, the weather was just terrible, and my muscles tied up like so many cords of rope. Just before the 1500-meter, it really turned bad. A few days earlier, I think I could have run some six seconds faster. I just couldn't get my legs loosened up for the race and ready to go," he says.

"There was just no way to win. I did the best with what I had; that's what I always did. Normally, I could have run away from Lovelock (New Zealand) in that last 300 yards. Jack Lovelock and I both broke existing records in that race. I finished second.

"Hitler didn't have much to do with the Olympics," Cunningham says. "He had a box in the stands and came in on schedule. The Olympic Committee set strict rules concerning political involvement.

"After the Olympics, we went to London," he remembers. "I did some running there, but didn't do too well. From London, we did a tour in Sweden. I had been there before when the American team had gone to Europe in 1933. At that time there was a masseur who had worked on my legs. We arrived in Stockholm late at night, and I called and asked him if he could come over the next morning and work on me, because I was having difficulty getting ready for the meet.

"He said, 'I know your legs—you need me tonight!' He came down and spent about an hour working on me, and then he showed up again the next morning. I really felt good and went out to win the 1500 meters going away, and came back with a new world's record in the half mile."

Back in New York, Cunningham and Jesse Owens were invited to a recording studio for a radio interview. They walked through the hotel lobby to the elevator, but the operator said that Jesse would have to use the freight elevator.

Cunningham said, "If this elevator isn't good enough for him, it's not good enough for me." They started to leave, but hadn't reached the door before the hotel decided that Jesse could take the regular elevator.

"Jesse was one of the finest human beings I've ever known," Cunningham says. "He was a gentleman, and he came up the hard way, from a poor family. I always appreciated his friendship."

When the '36 Olympic Games were over, Cunningham decided to

further his education. "There was another reason," he says. "I didn't have enough money to get back to Kansas! So right after we landed in New York, I enrolled in New York University, in the doctoral program."

Cunningham earned a master's degree in education from the University of Iowa and a doctorate in education from New York University, but said he was more proud of the calluses on his hands from hard work than of any degree he'd earned.

At the Memphis Invitational in 1937 Cunningham, who had taken an exam at NYU at 11 in the morning, didn't arrive in Tennessee until 6:30 in the evening. Two hours later, he won the mile on an empty stomach and, according to sports writers, "one sock-less foot."

"I did competitive running all through my doctoral studies," Cunningham says. "For a couple of years after graduation, I was at the University of Kansas traveling and doing public relations work for them. They about ran the legs off me, and the tires off the car. I was averaging 500 miles a week, most of it on country roads. There was one indoor season when I never stepped on a track for a workout. My workouts were the races.

"I'll tell you," Cunningham says, "I was bull-headed sometimes, and ran in races where I had no business running. In high school, when we were going to Chicago, the doctors told me not to go because I had a blister on my heel. I went anyway and did a lot of walking. I wanted to see the Boston Red Sox play the White Sox.

"The result of not taking care of myself was that I got blood poisoning. I went to the hospital on Wednesday, and my temperature was 104 degrees. I was told to drink a lot of ice water and fruit juices. But I didn't eat anything from that Wednesday night until after I ran the following Saturday.

"That morning my fever was 102 degrees, and my doctor would not release me from the hospital. I told him I was going to run, but they wouldn't get me my clothes. They decided to get my coach and if he agreed, he would have to sign a release relieving them of all responsibility. 'If you go out there and run,' they said, 'you could drop dead on the track.'

"I went out there and ran, and it was the only race I lost in high school. I shouldn't have run. I was so weak afterward that the coach had to hold me up in that Chicago wind.

"Athletics was fun for me," Cunningham says, "but it was never the first thing. When I was in New York working on the Ph.D., I spent my spare time down in the slum areas. There were allegedly over 400 cellar clubs, gangs of kids in different communities. They would find some old building, such as a deserted basement, and use it as a hangout.

"I would go down and visit, and because they'd heard about me running in Madison Square Garden, they thought if I took an interest in them, I was all right. We talked to local merchants about putting in lighting and fixing abandoned buildings with basketball goals and the like. During the spring we would have field days and I would go out and run with them.

"They thought it was the greatest thing, to run a race with me. I'd just jog along and have a good time. I wouldn't run away from anybody, because I didn't want to embarrass any of them.

"I never could understand why people who are competing in the same event couldn't be friends," he says. "In so many sports, competitors resent each other. It was different in track. I was friendly with everyone I competed against, and some of the strongest are my best friends.

"Winning the race was important," Cunningham says, "but I was never much interested in setting records. Runners who go out to set records often don't last long.

"I used to talk to some of my friends and try to help them with their running—pointing out how they could correct something that would help them compete better. Some people thought I was stupid for doing that, saying that the people I helped would come back and beat me. But I always thought that if I could make my competitor better, then I would get better. If I was going to win, I had to improve myself constantly."

Cunningham's love and respect for his fellow human beings extended to a genuine affection for animals. "I grew up with animals," he says, "horses, mules, cattle, dogs, a burro and ponies to ride. All of them were my friends and I learned a lot from them.

"There were a lot of coyote hounds out here in Western Kansas," Cunningham says, "but there were also greyhounds and those big old Russian wolfhounds that could tear a coyote to pieces right quick. Well, I had a little ol' dog that would defend me against anything, and he would grab one of those big dogs, chew on their foot and they would take off!"

Cunningham also had ground squirrels and rabbits for pets. "I started herding cattle when I was about six," he says. "One day when I was herding, I heard this little rabbit squealing to beat the band, because this darn snake was starting to swallow him. I took the bridle off my pony and hit the snake until he let go. Then I took the rabbit home and raised him.

"Many times the dogs would chase a coyote and it would go into its den. When we dug it out, we'd find a pair of pups that we'd take home and make pets out of them." Of one particular pair, Cunningham remembers, "the female didn't like men, but you could leave a little baby with it and she would love it and take care of it. She would never bite any of the kids; she just didn't like men.

"The old dog coyote just liked everybody, like a regular friendly old dog. I used to grab him by the jowls and shake him around, to play with him. People would think he was going to eat me. I'd throw him away, and he'd grab my arm. We used to take him out and he would run ahead and hide in some tall grass. Then when we came by he would jump up and grab us by the arm. We had so much fun with him.

"I always loved animals and couldn't enjoy hunting at all. I don't like killing anything and wouldn't, unless I was just desperate for food. Kindness and consideration of living things shows the character of an individual more than anything else. You take a person who doesn't like a dog, and they probably don't like people, either. I would go without food to buy feed for the animals. I don't know how many stray dogs I have brought home. My children are the same way. It was this closeness with animal life that brought about our idea for the Youth Ranch."

Cunningham served in the Navy during World War II, and was responsible for establishing new physical training programs at the Great Lakes and San Diego training stations.

Cunningham retired from racing in 1940 and served as director of physical education at Cornell College in Iowa.

Glenn and Ruth Cunningham settled on an 840-acre ranch north of Wichita after Glenn's wartime service in the Navy. He was an inspirational speaker in demand for commencements, clubs, schools and churches. His positive message of "You can do it!" often brought parents to him, seeking help for the problems they had with their children. Glenn began inviting troubled youngsters to stay at the ranch, where they joined the Cunningham family for a few days, weeks or even for years. This was the Glenn Cunningham Youth Ranch, where they helped to raise underprivileged children for 30 years. Accepting no federal or state funds, they supported the operation of the ranch from Cunningham's lecture tours around the United States.

The well-known author of the book *Never Quit*, Cunningham was featured in *Reader's Digest* (February 1966, April 1982, November 1989); *The Saturday Evening Post* (written by Jesse Owens, April 1976); and countless sports magazines and newspaper articles.

The Cunninghams had six daughters and four sons of their own, but managed to keep the ranch bills paid through Glenn's speaking tours. The ranch was closed in 1978. However, it reopened in 1985 as Glenhaven Youth Ranch in honor of the man who donated land for the ranch and helped support the work of two young couples who would continue the Cunninghams' work with at-risk young people.

Ken West, a young man who recounted his experience at the ranch in a *Reader's Digest* article, says that he was given his own horse and told that he was responsible for it. Like all the other children in the Cunningham's care, he was expected to work hard in school, help with chores, and follow the rules.

Years later, West still remembers the things Cunningham told the youngsters at the ranch, among them: "Laughter builds strength in the soul, and without muscle in the soul, you can't face the tough things in life."

He also remembered Cunningham saying that "if you have a tune in your heart, you owe the world a song," which gave West the inspiration to begin his own business. A favorite parable told by Glenn was of two men who saw a river. One saw it as a problem, the other a challenge. "Guess who gets to the other side first?" Cunningham would ask.

West says that Glenn's philosophy was not to give up on children— that there was good in all of them. He believed it was his job to "help them find it and let it shine through."

Hundreds of troubled children received a warm welcome at the Cunningham home in the form of love, attention, clothing, food, discipline and guidance to be the best they could be. Each learned to do their share of duties and assume responsibility for their behavior and the well-being of others.

"We have never directed any of our children into athletics," Cunningham says. "If they wanted to become an athlete, we encouraged them to do so. I never interfered with their training, because I wanted my children to be fully responsible to their coaches. However, if I worked with them, they often had better results." It was Cunningham's belief that each runner was an individual and should have training that suited their specific needs. Glenn Jr. ran the mile and two mile at the University of Kansas. He ran a 4:13 mile. During his senior year, he never lost a race—outdoors, indoors or cross-country.

Asked about the current sports scene, Cunningham says that he's always believed in strong discipline for athletes. "When a coach has players who break training rules, he has the right to drop them off as they did here in Arkansas a few years back. They were some of the best players, but the team went ahead and won a Bowl game without them.

"Training techniques and the synthetic tracks have really improved performance," Cunningham says. "A few years back when I was a little over 70, Jim Ryun, **Wes Santee** and I were invited to the Kansas Relays where we were to run a victory lap. Santee lived near the University and had been working out, Ryun hadn't been running, and I hadn't done even much jogging. I told them I didn't know if I could go a quarter of a mile.

"They gave us new equipment, and I put on these shoes. My God, they were different than anything I had ever worn before! When we got out on the track, it was so springy, I couldn't believe it.

"We started out, with Santee picking up the pace and Ryun and I keeping right up. I don't know if they timed us or not, but it was a pretty good quarter mile. Those shoes felt like they had helium in them! I could hardly keep them on the track, because they just floated there, and I didn't even draw a long breath at the finish!"

Cunningham claimed to never have smoked or drunk either coffee or alcohol. Later in life he was a spokesperson for the Temperance Tornado movement, which opposed the repeal of Prohibition in Kansas.

In 1939, Cunningham asked fans at the Pennsylvania Athletic Club Indoor track meet in Philadelphia not to light up cigarettes. Cunningham believed that the less smoke, the faster the winning time. Fans usually complied. He was still able to win 22 indoor mile races at the smoke-filled Madison Square Garden.

Cunningham won the Wanamaker Mile Championship six times. The Wanamaker Mile, part of the Millrose Games, is named for Rodman Wanamaker, head of the once-famous Wanamaker Department Store in New York City. The Wanamaker Mile is run at 10 o'clock in the evening, a tradition that began when sports announcer Ted Husing broadcast the race live during the nightly news.

3

John Kenneth "Ken" Doherty

DECATHLON • BRONZE MEDAL
Born May 16, 1905, Detroit, Michigan
Died April 17, 1996, Lancaster, Pennsylvania

Ken Doherty achieved fame, both as a decathlete and as a longtime coach at the University of Michigan and the University of Pennsylvania. A graduate of Wayne State University in Detroit, Michigan, he won two national AAU decathlon championships (1928, 1929), setting an American record. In 1928, he won the bronze medal in the decathlon at the Amsterdam Games.

He was an assistant coach at Princeton, and moved on to be head coach at the University of Michigan from 1939 to 1948, where his athletes won nine Big Ten team titles.

In the early 1950s, Doherty moved to the University of Pennsylvania where he directed the Penn Relays, the *Philadelphia Inquirer* indoor meet, the first USA–USSR dual track meet, and the AAU Championships in 1961. In 1953 he wrote his first track and field textbook, *Modern Track and Field.*

When he retired from coaching, Doherty wrote the classic *Track and Field Omnibook,* a training book that instructed and inspired a generation of coaches.

Career Achievements

- At the 1928 Olympic trials in Cambridge, Massachusetts, Doherty placed first in the decathlon with 7,600.52 points.

Ken Doherty (decathlon). (Courtesy the Walter Reuther Library, Wayne State University.)

- When he was head track coach at the University of Michigan (1940–1948) Doherty's track teams won four Big Ten Indoor Titles and three Big Ten Outdoor titles.

- His teams won 30 event titles in the Big Ten Indoor, 18 in the Big Ten Outdoor, and seven in the NCAA Outdoor meets.

- Doherty was elected to the Helms Track and Field Hall of Fame in 1961.

- He was enshrined in the Michigan Track and Field Hall of Fame in 1970, the United States Track and Field Hall of Fame in 1976, and the Wayne State Athletic Hall of Fame in 1977.

- Doherty was inducted into Class II of the Penn Athletic Hall of Fame (University of Pennsylvania) in 1998.

- He was president of the National College Track Coaches Association.

- In 1933, Doherty earned an M.A. in Education from the University of Michigan, and a Ph.D. in Education from the same institution in 1949.

- He published articles in track and field trade journals, and was one of the leading authors of the sport for three decades.

- The Ken Doherty Memorial Fellowship was established to encourage research and publication in track and field. It provides travel, room and board for its recipients to conduct research at the National Track and Field Hall of Fame in Los Angeles. The fellowship especially encourages research and publication that addresses philosophical, social, historical, or psychological issues related to sport.

Interview

"A runner's creed: I will win; if I cannot win, I shall be second; if I cannot be second, I shall be third; if I cannot place at all, I shall still do my best."—Ken Doherty

Interviewer's Notes

My visit with Ken Doherty was more than I could have anticipated. We did discuss track and field, and some of the world class athletes he had coached at the University of Michigan. But the interview also included areas of human understanding, because it focused heavily on the youth camps he had developed. He enjoyed his work with these camps as much as his coaching experience with athletes.

I had lunch with Ken, who served a homemade stew, while we listened to an hourlong tape of loons, one of many recorded at one of his camps in Michigan. Later he took me upstairs and showed me his paintings of landscapes and wildlife, a hobby he had taken up with great pleasure.

In the same room were a stack of sealed boxes. "I have to get these shipped to the track and field library," he said.

I ask him about his early experiences with athletics.

* * * * *

"I first became aware of sports when I was about six," he says, "because the local pole vault champion lived across the street. I took my mother's clothes pole, and tried to clear a string stretched across two fence posts.

"At that time, I didn't know what 'track and field' meant," he adds, "but when we lived in Petosky, Michigan, there were several of us that were interested in running, and we held contests for running around the block. The neighbor children and I unloaded things from our attics and set them up as prizes."

Doherty remembers being small for his age. "At the end of high school," he says, "they gave me a letter for long and faithful service!"

"I was quite independent," Doherty says. "I worked when I was in college. Tuition at that time was $35 a semester."

Doherty didn't realize that he had any real athletic potential until his junior year in college. "I went out for track and field because my friend Stan was a pole vaulter at Detroit City College under Coach David Holmes," Doherty says. (In 1933 Detroit City College was incorporated into Wayne University, which became Wayne State University in 1956.)

"We did nothing well. For example, my freshman year I jumped 5'8" and threw the javelin about 135 feet. If I pole vaulted at all, it would have been eight or nine feet. But, because it was fun and there was little other talent on the team, we tried all the events," he remembers. "In the course of a few years, Coach Holmes developed quite a track team.

"I'm not sure my father knew I was out for a sport, because he didn't have an interest at that time in either college or sport." Doherty says that his mother was interested, but her participation was limited, with five children in the family to care for. During the National Championships after his senior year, and then the Olympics, his parents began attending the events.

"Each of my coaches was different," he says. "Our high school coach was a Turnverein. Sport was not an important affair and training on the squad was unorganized." Doherty remembers his coach as a disciplinarian, and one who followed a military methodology in his teaching. "We really didn't train," he says, "we just took part. There wasn't any progression from early season until late."

Turnvereins or "turners" were gymnastics organizations that originated in Germany in the early 1800s. The program fell in and out of popularity with changing social conditions in Germany, but became popular in the U.S. after gymnastics were included in the 1896 Olympics. Later, the highly regimented gymnastics program was used in military training and adopted into the physical education curricula of U.S. schools. The program stressed the development of strength and power in men, and grace and movement for women.

Asked to address the changing conditions of an athlete's social behavior, Doherty says, "We were very conscious in the 1920s of the things we shouldn't do, but we were told very little about what we could do that was positive. There were a lot of 'Thou shalt nots.' We weren't even supposed to kiss a girl, because we might catch some serious disease."

Doherty remembers another "Thou shalt not" of the period. "The Volstead people were extremely active in the church," he says. (Andrew Volstead, a member of the House of Representatives, was the author of the National Prohibition Act, also known as the Volstead Act, passed by Congress in 1919. The law prohibited the manufacture, transportation and sale of beverages containing more than 0.5 per cent alcohol.) "Mother insisted that I go with her to church where the evils of alcohol were a major interest. I never had one drop until after the Olympic Games in Amsterdam in 1928–29, when I had a glass of beer," he laughs.

"There was also a great emphasis on the dangers of doing too much," Doherty says. "In a *Saturday Evening Post* article on the subject of over-work, a coach wrote that he had some fine distance runners at Penn and his job was to chase them off the track!

"Coach Holmes was my only coach in college," Doherty says. "He came out from Oklahoma and had no competition experience. There were no textbooks in those days. In 1925 the AAU came out with a series of books on track and field, and I don't believe there was an athletic journal. But Holmes was a great innovator. We didn't have examples, so every event was experimental. I was trying to throw the discus five different ways."

"There didn't seem to be the need for imposed discipline," Doherty remembers. "We were out for fun, a sweater, and maybe a medal or two. There was no press other than our school paper.

"From the age of 14 or 15, I knew I was going to college and I wanted to teach English. After I graduated from Wayne State University, I went to the University of Michigan to better myself for the Olympics and to get courses to qualify for an English Teaching Certificate.

"In 1929 I got an opportunity to coach at Princeton," Doherty says, "although coaching was not my main goal. My primary interest was English literature. The why and how of athletics always interested me more than the practice. I became acquainted with Brutus Hamilton and thought he was a top man, but not because he was winning. He was just a great man."

As a sophomore at the University of Missouri, Brutus Hamilton was national decathlon champion in 1920 and silver medal decathlete at the Olympics the same year. He lost the gold to a Norwegian soldier, Helge Lövland, by the smallest margin recorded in the Olympic decathlon. He was track coach at UCLA from 1932 to 1965, and decathlete coach for the U.S. Olympic team in 1932 and 1936. He was head coach of the men's track team that won 14 gold medals at the 1952 Olympics. He coached **Glenn Cunningham,** the world's fastest miler in 1938, and Don Bowden, the first American to break the four-minute mile.

"We did not do well in the '28 Olympics," Doherty says. "I believe we really came to life in 1932. Coaches went to the Olympics as spectators and became aware of techniques. Studies and research go back to 1932."

Doherty remembers that there were no track and field training camps in 1928. Instead, "We were told to be at the dock and get on the boat. The athletes got together at the Paramount Hotel in New York City and then went to the boat—that was our training camp. We had nothing organized in the way of conditioning on the ship.

"It was almost as bad in Holland. We had no training program prior to the games. Our coach was a fine fellow, but he pretty much stood around and we did as we pleased. I don't know how much he knew about track and field, but I don't think he believed in coaching at the Olympics. By that time, he felt, it was too late for coaching."

When Doherty was asked about what athletic participation had meant to him, he replied, "Sports have had an extremely strong influence in my life, but almost by the back door, in a secondary way. My real interest in life, and a great influence to me personally, has been operating recreational camps. I was into canoe camping for many years. That kind of experience out of doors, away from the city and civilization, has meant more to me in my life than any other experience including athletics. In the past few years I have taken up painting, and have painted trees, water, sky and birds—that sort of thing."

Doherty says, "There is civilization and a society on the one hand, and the individual and local environment on the other. The two are inseparable. There is no way that the individual can develop on his own what he believes or hopes to accomplish. It is always done in terms of the greater environment, the greater whole.

"In my own lifetime," he adds, "I am extremely aware of how much the attitudes of the culture in general and those of my neighbors, friends, and associates have changed. It's not exactly a 180 turn but it is certainly 90 degrees or more!

"Seventy-five years ago our culture seemed to have no clearcut purpose or shared interests. We weren't sure what we wanted to become, and we tended to be quite isolated—one city from another; one small town or group from another. Our attitudes and experiences were mainly influenced by our neighborhood.

"There was little interest in knowing what was happening in other towns when I was young, even in the city of Detroit, which was only 200 miles away. New York, Paris, and Rome were dots on a map. Religion was local; educational attitudes were local; everything we thought about and believed in seemed no larger than our own circle of acquaintances."

Doherty sees the position of the individual in today's society as very different. He believes that the country has moved to the opposite extreme: away from valuing the individual to a point where people lose their identity and their uniqueness. What is expected from young people has changed from individual interests to a more determined progression through school and into a career.

"People who attend college must go to learn a vocation," he says, "not to learn about themselves and the world. Anyone who doesn't go with that purpose is not very realistic. In our culture today, the individual is almost overwhelmed.

"At one time in our history, sports were fun, and we did it if we enjoyed doing it," Doherty says. "If you won a medal—that was great. Being paid for it in my day was despicable. That was the kind of thing wrestlers and boxers did.

"When I was a boy, there was no professional football or basketball. In the past few years, the shift in attitude toward the professional, and toward moneymaking as a result of sport, has been tremendous," Doherty says.

He disagrees with the practice of major sports publications pushing for professional sports. "They always said they were pushing against the hypocrisy, but the effect of their writing has been toward more acceptance of sport as a profession.

"In all fairness," Doherty adds, "a good argument can be put for that point of view. If it is honorable to earn your money in other ways, why shouldn't it be by running and jumping?"

Doherty notes that there has always been hypocrisy in amateur athletics. "The English in the late 1880s were the chief proponents of amateurism," he says. "Most of the writing of the international rules relating to amateurism was done by the English."

He notes the exception of the Sheffield Handicap in England—100- and 220-yard races in the 1890s. "Various Americans competed in these professional races in England," Doherty says. "Although England was the chief amateur, they also had their professionals."

Doherty believes that track and field will go along with what happens to the other sports, and sports will follow the pattern of the culture as a whole. "That is what they have always done," he says, "and they will continue to do so, more and more.

"What happens to the culture as a whole with this emphasis on commercialism?" Doherty asks. "We cannot go on in a narrow-minded way, focusing on just one aspect—money, and more money. I assume some kind of a collapse will happen. The top, as it is, cannot be maintained."

Doherty is saddened by the decrease in the number of track and field courses offered at U.S. colleges. "Sport for the fun of it," he says, "is gone. Participation now focuses on winning a championship or making money. You do it for what you can get out of it.

"It would be difficult for me to explain what athletics have meant to me," he says. "Sport is one way of learning how to demand more from yourself by concentrating on a role—running, jumping, whatever it is. But this goal could as easily be achieved by playing the violin. Youngsters who attend our music camps go on stage alone, accompanied by an orchestra. In front of several thousands in the audience, they perform for prizes, such as a chair in the orchestra or scholarships.

"I admire the achievements of these youngsters as much as any I've seen perform at a track meet. It can be an emotional experience. But I have also had these powerful emotions as a coach, when I've been deeply impressed by a great performance.

"Back in the 1920s," Doherty remembers, "you could count the marathoners on your fingers. Long distance runs were the mile and two mile. We had not heard of the 5000-meter or 10,000-meter runs. Distance runners trained at minimal levels. We really didn't get interested in these races until the late '30s," he says, "when Billy Hayes of Indiana went to Finland and Sweden and saw how the Scandinavian runners were training year around with increasing distances and increasing pace."

Hall of Fame coach Earl "Billy" Hayes was track coach at Indiana University from 1925 until 1943. He championed distance running and influenced the training of runners worldwide. He coached some of the best distance runners in U.S. history.

"He came back to this country and developed those great runners at Indiana: Don Lash and Chuck Hornbostel," Doherty says. "Because of their superior performances, other coaches started thinking about 'doing more,' rather than the old theory of 'doing less.' Previously, the emphasis had been on achieving as much as you could with the least output of energy. The more hours of sleep you got, the better.

"In 1941 I was in California for a NCAA Championship Meet, and the Swedish National coach and I went out for a walk. We were just talking track and field when he said, 'Ken, the most amazing thing to me is that during the last hour we have seen no one jog and very few people out walking.'

"In California," Doherty observes, "you never saw people jogging in those days. You didn't even see many people walking. When the coach mentioned it to me, I was shocked. I hadn't even noticed. I had taken it for granted that if someone wanted to go somewhere, they got in an automobile. They didn't walk, and certainly no one would be jogging.

"In the early 1950s," Doherty continues, "Bill Bowerman started his jogging program." Bowerman was head track coach at Oregon University for 24 years. Co-founder of the Nike company, he designed their first running shoe and wrote a popular book on jogging. Bowerman trained some of the great U.S. distance runners and increased the popularity of the sport.

"Not only did Bowerman give his runners far greater distances than other coaches around the country," Doherty says, "Oregon became the leading distance running school in the country. Bowerman also started jogging himself. He got some medical doctors to jog with him and they became interested. I was one of the early members of the National Association of Sports Medicine and worked my way up to vice president.

"The medical profession was shocked at the degree to which the track coaches were pushing their runners in terms of output of energy. It was a shock to the medical profession as a whole when a few doctors at the Harvard Fatigue Laboratory began to do experiments that indicated a healthy heart was one that could be used at the higher levels.

"Jogging seems to have taken over as a sport that has no concern about winning or making money," Doherty says. "I don't see this kind of thing taking place in football, except perhaps for touch football. In basketball, which is a fun game, I see some real potential.

"Until fairly recent times," Doherty says, "most coaches did not receive scientific training. Most learned by doing and what they gathered from their own coaches. They did not learn their coaching techniques from biomechanics or physiology. Some of the old books on physiology of exercise make one laugh.

Doherty's book, *Track and Field Omnibook* (1976), was the first comprehensive book written for coaching track and field. It not only included the basic techniques of instruction, but introduced elements of sport psychology and motivation.

Doherty says that his second job in coaching was at the University of Michigan, beginning in 1931 under Charles White. "He was a great sprinter at Grinnell," Doherty adds, "and held the world's record at 220 yards. He did not make the Olympic team, however, perhaps because of the war.

"Charley White was a dual meet coach. (Individual event wins at a track meet are assigned scores that produce a team score). He believed in large teams and we actually had 'B' team dual meets. When he was at Michigan, he never lost a dual meet during his last four or five years. We won most of the Big Ten Championships.

"Each year we considered the events in which we were weak. We never took a team attitude toward National Competition. We never asked the question 'Could we win the National championship?' Our dual meet season was climaxed by the Big Ten meet and our season was over. We held the team meeting, took pictures, elected the captain, and then dispersed."

Doherty says that the coach told them if any of them wanted to go on to the National Championships, he would be happy to work with them. "A few would go, which is a big difference from what happens now. So many colleges that have won the NCAA meet in the past 20 years have won because they have a few champions, some who have been imported.

"Bill Bowerman was one of the few exceptions. Bill was probably the last of the dual meet coaches. I have example after example where athletes have written to me about winning a fifth place and how much it meant to them."

Doherty's third stint in coaching track and field was at the University of Pennsylvania, beginning in the early 1950s, where he brought new life to the Penn Relays.

The first Penn Relays were held on April 21, 1895, and are now the longest uninterrupted collegiate track meet in the country. The first Penn Relays in 1895 drew a crowd of 5,000 spectators, the largest up to that time in Philadelphia. In 1920 the Penn Relays included a combined team from Oxford and Cambridge universities, and drew a crowd of more than 30,000, with thousands more turned away. Neither university could field an entire team, because almost a generation of young athletes had been killed or wounded in World War I. More athletes have participated in the Penn Relays than in any other single meet in the world. More spectators have watched the meet than any in the world except the Olympics.

During his tenure, he increased the size of the track used for the meet, adding six lanes to the inside of the track, which could be used for sprints. This improvement increased the number of athletes who could participate in the competition, made it easier for spectators to see the races from the stands, and provided a better running surface, since the inner tracks would not have received as much wear from the longer distance races.

Doherty added competitive events for postcollegiate athletes, which became known as the Olympic Development events. He increased the efficiency of the Relays by turning the northwest corner of the track into the clerking area. This new organization of the field allowed more athletes to participate, increased interest in the events, and provided better viewing opportunities for spectators.

Doherty also scheduled the major events of the Relays on Saturday afternoon, which proved to be a popular move for spectators. In 1956, the crowd exceeded 35,000 for the first time, with 4,000 athletes participating. By 1958, the crowd exceeded 43,000.

After Ken Doherty retired, he became involved in the Organized Summer Camp Movement. He was a volunteer at the famed camp for young musicians in Interlochen, Michigan.

When the Track and Field Hall of Fame Library was established at Butler University in Indianapolis, Indiana, Dr. Doherty donated his entire track and field collection to the library. The library holdings at that time included thousands of books, periodicals, and manuscripts related to the history of track and field in America. Because of space limitations, the collection was moved in 2001 to the Amateur Athletic Foundation headquarters in Los Angeles, where much of the data is made available online to researchers throughout the world. The collection joins the substantial AAF collection, which includes 35,000 printed volumes, 90,000 photo images, 8,000 microform volumes and 6,000 videos.

4

Richard Douglas "Dick" Fosbury

HIGH JUMP • GOLD MEDAL
Born March 6, 1947, Portland, Oregon

Best known for his technique of clearing the bar with a twisting backwards somersault dubbed the "Fosbury flop," Dick Fosbury was the surprise gold medal winner in the high jump event at Mexico City in 1968, where he jumped 7'4¼", for American and Olympic records.

The 21-year-old athlete, coached by the legendary **Berny Wagner** at Oregon State University, faced the sky instead of the bar as he crossed it, to win America its first gold medal in the event since 1956. Fosbury also won the NCAA championships in 1968 and 1969, and was ranked top jumper in the world after his win in Mexico City.

Most jumpers of Fosbury's time used the straddle or "belly roll" method: going over the crossbar with their lead arm and leg, and then their stomach. Despite Fosbury's extraordinary performance using the "flop," it did not catch on for a number of years, because most jumpers had invested a career lifetime in perfecting the straddle.

Career Achievements

- Fosbury began using the "flop" when he was sixteen, and improved his best jump at 5 feet 3¾ inches to 6 feet 6¾ inches within two years.

- As a straddle jumper in high school, Fosbury never cleared higher than 5'4". When he began use the technique that eventually evolved into the "flop," Fosbury improved his height to 5'10".

Dick Fosbury (high jump). (Courtesy Berny Wagner.)

- By his senior year, Fosbury was clearing over six feet with his unorthodox jump.

- In 1965, the summer after he graduated from high school, Fosbury won the National Junior Chamber of Commerce Championship with a 6'7" jump.

- Fosbury was the first ever to jump over seven feet indoors at an NCAA meet.

- During the 1968 collegiate indoor season, Fosbury cleared 7'1¼."

- In the outdoor season of 1968, he raised his personal best to 7'2¼" and won the National Collegiate title.

- Fosbury finished third at the Olympic trial finals at Lake Tahoe in September with a personal best of 7'3".

- Fosbury was elected to the Track and Field Hall of Fame in 1981 and the U.S. Olympic Hall of Fame in 1992.

- On the 30th anniversary of his extraordinary performance at the Mexico City Olympics, Fosbury won the bronze at the World Masters competition in Eugene, Oregon.

Interview

*"I was fortunate to grow up in America, which allows this atti-
tude to evolve in athletic competition—to break out of the norm,
as long as there is success."*

Interviewer's Notes

A reporter at the Olympics asked Fosbury what he called his revolutionary jumping technique. Fosbury remembered a newspaper headline
from his high school days: "Fosbury Flops over the Bar." He told the
reporter, "It's called the Fosbury Flop."

When I visited with Dick Fosbury, who was an engineer by profession, I asked him how he applied mechanical rules to "the flop." His
answer was that the technique evolved when he started thinking about
the best way to get over the bar, when he was in junior high.

At training camp I never saw Dick Fosbury jump, because it was his
routine to save his best efforts for competition and not leave his good
jumps in practice. This contrasted with the routines of other jumpers who
saw practice as a rehearsal, but no one could argue with Fosbury's results.

He did work with a few throwers who wanted to experiment with
the jump. Out on the field, you could see three-hundred-pound hammer
throwers and shot putters trying out the flop.

Celebrities from Hollywood also came and went during the training period at Lake Tahoe. Danny Kaye (movie star, world ambassador for
UNICEF) walked all around the practice fields watching how the jumps
were done.

Jerry Van Dyke (*Coach*, movies) and Don Knotts (*Andy Griffith Show*,
movies) were on the bill at Harrah's nearby. They gave the athletes and their
coaches free tickets for the show, and we had front row seats. Don Knotts
remembered the names of the athletes and introduced them to the crowd.

On a guest spot on *The Tonight Show*, Fosbury jumped with Bill
Cosby and the show's host Johnny Carson, who impressed him by
"flopping" four feet without a running approach.

* * * * *

When I asked Dick Fosbury how he came to know about sports, he
said, "I lived in the country, and the first school I went to had just six
grades. My first encounters with sport were the usual playground games,
like tag. Later I attended a large school with hundreds of kids, and it was
there I discovered that I had a very competitive personality. I was natu-

rally shy and found that competition in sports was an easy way to get to know people.

"I discovered at an early age that I had a talent for mathematics, and I was particularly interested in science. I also enjoyed music, especially singing, and sang in the choir through high school. With regard to athletic ability, I was always in the middle—just an average kid. I played all the sports but didn't feel very comfortable in baseball. I was always a tall kid and was attracted to basketball. I participated in track and field and, although I was never exceptional, I was competitive and could win a few events."

Asked to describe how he developed the "Fosbury Flop," he says, "When I was ten or eleven, the teacher taught us how to do the Western roll, the straddle, and the scissors technique, which was antiquated. I was attracted to the scissors form, because I was tall, and it was more natural to keep my body upright and try to jump straight up.

"I believe that when you are learning a new event, instinct takes over. You may not have the confidence to raise the bar above your head, but if the bar is only waist high, you immediately pick up bad habits. You learn to jump down *at* the bar, which is bad technique in the Western roll and the straddle. But you just practice that, and eventually your physical skills begin to catch up."

Dick Fosbury was 6'3" tall and weighed 160 pounds when he competed. He considered himself gangly and uncoordinated. Of the "Flop," Fosbury said, "My mind wanted me to get over the bar, and intuitively it figured out the most efficient way to do it."

Many doctors at the time expressed concern about the twisting backward somersault technique. However, jumpers using the "Flop" correctly land on their shoulders, not on their necks. Air bags and sponge mats have greatly increased the safety of the "Flop." By 1980, more than three quarters of the Olympic finalists were using the "Fosbury Flop."

"In high school, you begin to challenge yourself, and try to jump above your head, he continued his explanation. "I was a sophomore and had been using the old style of jumping. The 'Fosbury Flop' was a natural style, which came about because of my desire to play the game. I actually developed the technique during competition, when my only conscious thought was getting over the bar.

"I talked with Parry O'Brien, world record holder in the shot put. He told me that he developed the technique of starting with his back to the toe board in the same way, as a natural effort to win.

"I think it is human nature to try different things," Fosbury says, "rather than to depend exclusively on a coach to guide us using set norms and standards. I was fortunate to grow up in America, which allows this attitude to evolve in athletic competition—to break out of the norm, as long as there is success.

"My first big splash using the flop was in 1967," he remembers, "in the NCAA meet at Brigham Young University. **Berny Wagner** had put me on a great strength program, and the results were beginning to bear out.

"Berny was very clever. When I first started at Oregon State, he and I talked about what my goals were. I told him I wanted to be the best high jumper that I could be. He had been a good straddle coach in junior college, and promised me that he would work with me and teach me what he knew of the straddle form.

"Because I had success coming into college, he felt it would be a good compromise to let me compete with my technique, and eventually the plan was that I would surpass my heights by learning how to do the straddle. No one had ever analyzed the Flop to see whether it had good efficiency or was a good technique.

"During spring break of my sophomore year," Fosbury says, "we traveled to sunny California for a meet. Out of the Oregon wind, I jumped 6'10", which was the school record. After the meet, Berny said, 'Let's bag this program you're on.' He wanted me to continue with my technique. He would analyze it, study it, and try to discover what made it work.

"Actually, I never practiced much on technique, and this drove Berny crazy! It wasn't normal. All I knew was that when I got into competition, I was psyched up, nervous—adrenaline was flowing. In practice, I didn't feel as focused, and made more errors than I did during competition.

"I guess I'm just the exception," he says. "Berny put me on a good strength program. He got me in the weight room with the throwers—shotput, discus and hammer. Those guys taught me the exercises and lifts they thought were appropriate for the high jump. These included squats, half and quarter leg extensors, leg presses, and leg pulls. Very simple stuff. There were also a few upper body exercises—those that would primarily work with leg strength. I credit weight training for my major success.

"I had always been attracted to plyometrics [depth jumping—stretching and bounding over things to improve flexibility and jumping ability]. My coach for this was George Chaplin, who later coached at Washington State and served as an Olympic Team Coach. He gave me more drills to do, and explained that a guy who was jumping better than me was doing certain types of bounding exercises.

"So I would go and hop stairs," Fosbury says, "about 20 rows in the basketball coliseum, hopping on one leg and then the other. I would do a couple of sets of these until I was shaking. I alternated those days of bounding exercises with the strength training.

"One of the things that always appealed to me was the fact that Berny was a strategist. (He had graduated as an engineer.) He would have meetings before competition and project the hypothetical results of the meet, based on our performance against the competition.

"Typically, we would get down to the last event and be behind by four or five points every time. It would always be close, so we knew that if we were going to win, we had to improve our goals. Just going through that session every weekend before the competition was really a tremendous motivator.

"When I first started out in college, I was faced with academic challenges and then track team workouts at the end of the day. I studied engineering, which was a difficult and challenging curriculum for me, and I was always trying to play catchup. A lot of the time I missed practice, but I always made my workouts.

"Berny called me into the office several times, wondering if I had quit the track team. He wanted to know what was going on. I couldn't keep up with the regular schedule, but I would still get in my regular workouts. I was just a freshman, and he didn't know if he could trust me. I know I drove him crazy.

"My parents got a divorce when I was in high school. It changed our family situation and was really difficult. My mother, as a single parent, had her hands full with me and my sister. I didn't see much of my dad, although he did come to a couple of basketball games and my track meets. These were usually held at the end of the work day, and he put in extra hours so he could come and watch me. He had played all sports when he was in high school, and from reading his yearbook I knew he had been a very good athlete.

"Most of my friends at that time were social," Fosbury says. "One of the most important interests we shared was chasing girls! We wanted to know what they were doing. I always had good friends on the team, but I didn't always socialize with them. I still keep in touch with a few high school buddies, and we chat about going to our next reunion. There are also college friends I keep in touch with, like a roommate back in Oregon.

"Philosophically, when you listen to the words of Pierre de Coubertin (founder of the modern Olympic Games), he really felt the Games would have an influence on society, because of the ideal of balance and moderation in all."

Fosbury remembers having conflicts with some of his coaches, who would keep him on the bench because he would occasionally miss a practice to sing in a performance.

"But I feel that balance is important in our society," he says. "When

I go out to teach the high jump to kids, I talk about balance in their life. Sport is only one part; you need those other things to develop your potential. I know how dedicated I was, but I always had other interests."

Fosbury's biggest concern with the Olympics is professionalism and cheating. "I grew up in the amateur era," he says, "but that doesn't necessarily mean that I believe that Avery Brundage's ideas should be followed today. Professionalism is in part a reflection of our society and culture, and it makes sense to include professional athletes in the Games."

Asked to respond to the current situation with drugs, Fosbury says that part of solving the problem is education. "We need to tell these young athletes what the risks are," he says. "I am still not an advocate of opening sports to every enhancement known to man, whether it is drugs or technology. It's obviously a big challenge, and a philosophical one. We should make rules and define the limits. Our game is on a track—it has lanes, and we have boundaries for what we do. I think we need athletes for models, with the message that to be a champion you don't have to take drugs."

5

William Bruce Jenner

DECATHLON • GOLD MEDAL
Born 1949, Mount Kisco, New York

Bruce Jenner competed in football, basketball, water skiing, and track and field in high school. He earned a football scholarship to attend Graceland College (now Graceland University) in Lamoni, Iowa. He was sidelined by a knee injury his freshman year; this accident eventually moved him into track and field and the decathlon.

Jenner won the 1971 NAIA decathlon championship and placed third in the Drake Relays in 1972. This qualified him for the Olympic Games in Munich, where he came in tenth in the field. Jenner devoted the next four years to training and competing, winning national championships in 1974 and 1976, and the Pan American Games decathlon championship in 1975 at Mexico City.

In 1976, Jenner won the gold at the Olympic Games in Montreal, Quebec, Canada, and set a new world's record. He retired after the Olympics to work in the entertainment industry, often lending his efforts and celebrity to noteworthy causes.

Career Achievements

- In high school, Jenner was all-state pole vault and high jump champion. He was also the Eastern United States water-skiing champion.

- Jenner competed in the Kansas University Relays, representing Graceland College. He won the decathlon title in 1971, and his winning 8,240 points in 1974 stood as a record until 1983.

- Jenner was given the Sullivan Award in 1976 for outstanding performance as an amateur athlete.

- The same year (1976), he was named Male Athlete of the Year by the Associated Press.

- He was inducted into the Track and Field Hall of Fame in 1980, and the Olympic Hall of Fame in 1986.

- Jenner was named to the Connecticut Hall of Fame in 1994.

- He was honored by the U.S. Jaycees as one of the Ten Outstanding Young Men in America.

- He is the author of *Finding the Champion Within* (Simon and Schuster, 1996).

- Jenner's first book, *Decathlon Challenge: Bruce Jenner's Story*, was on the American Library Association's list of "Best Books for Young Adults" in 1977.

- *Bruce Jenner's Viewer's Guide to the Olympics*, first published in 1980, was updated for the 1984 Summer Olympics.

- Jenner's *The Teenage Guide to Fitness* was published in 1984.

- Since he retired from competition, Jenner has appeared on television as an actor, producer, sports commentator, celebrity personality, commercial spokesperson, talk-show guest, and for seven years guest host and special correspondent for *Good Morning America*.

- Jenner has been a commentator for NBC Sports, ABC Sports, and Fox Sports, covering track and field events, surfing and motocross. He has served as a commentator during the Olympics, and was honored as Outstanding International Sportscaster of the Year in 1978.

- He appeared on the popular game shows, *The Weakest Link* and *Who Wants to Be a Millionaire?* to benefit his charities.

- Jenner was honored at a White House ceremony by the Lab School for Learning Disabilities, based in Washington, D.C.

- He received the Celebrity Outreach Award for his work in assisting charity fundraisers.

- He has his own fitness company, which promotes a healthy lifestyle, and is a well-respected motivational speaker.

Bruce Jenner and his dog, Bertha, who is wearing the Olympic medal. (Courtesy Bruce Jenner.)

• Jenner has served on the Council of Champions for the Special Olympics, the President's Council on Physical Fitness, and the California Governor's Council of Physical Fitness.

Interview

"Of all the things I did as a young kid, involvement in sports had the greatest impact on my life."

Interviewer's Notes

Bruce Jenner lived in Malibu, and since my sister JoAnn knew southern California like the back of her hand, she was my main source of transportation. When we reached Jenner's home, we were told that he would be on the ocean front at Malibu, watching his son participate in a softball game.

We found Bruce and sat in his automobile talking and watching the game. After a few innings, his son Brandon came up to the car a little green around the gills. He had eaten a hot dog with the works right before the game. The world's champion father promptly took him around the other side of the car to lend moral support, while Brandon got rid of the problem.

Bruce had the windows rolled down in the car, and every so often he'd yell "Go Brandon!" "Run, Brandon!" like any interested father. Then he would turn to me and ask "Where were we?" I could understand why he received several "Father of the Year" awards.

Bruce Jenner still has his boyish enthusiasm, the same spirit he displayed as the 1976 Olympic Decathlon Champion and world record holder. Today, as a television commentator, racing his sports car, cheering on his children in their various activities, or serving as a spokesperson for children and adults with dyslexia, Bruce still tackles things with intensity.

*****

"I was born in New York City," he begins, "and spent most of my early life in the New York–Westchester area."

Jenner, the second child in his family, grew up with two sisters and a brother in middle-class neighborhoods in New York and Connecticut. His father served in World War II and competed in the U.S. Army Olympics. In 1945, he won the silver medal in the 100-yard dash at the

U.S. Army Olympics in Nuremberg. Jenner's grandfather ran in the Boston Marathon for many years.

"If there was a single thing that influenced me during those developmental years," Jenner says, "it was growing up dyslexic. I had a very hard time in school, and really struggled. The simple task of reading was very difficult. My birthday is in October, so I started school just before my fifth birthday. I was a little immature for kindergarten—you know—screaming and crying and not wanting to go to school. All of that, combined with the dyslexia problem, made it a tough time.

"I started out with a very poor image of myself," he says, "especially intellectually. I always thought of myself as not too smart a kid. The biggest fear of my life, barring none," he remembers vividly, "was to read in front of the class—when the teacher would say: 'OK, you read the first paragraph and you read the second,' and so on.

"I was afraid to go to school," he says, "because I was afraid they would have me read in front of the class. There was always the fear that everyone would find out I was a dummy. In the 1950s, we didn't have the special reading classes, or anything like that. I was just stuck with my own problem, and didn't get much outside help."

Now Jenner lends his name and efforts to the National Dyslexia Research Foundation. He believes that dyslexia was a gift to him, because it motivated him to be the best at something that he could already do well. He was driven to overcome obstacles, and this translated into the intense focus he brought to competition. (Other famous people who have struggled with dyslexia include Albert Einstein, Thomas Edison, Jay Leno, Tom Cruise, and Cher.)

"In the fifth grade, however, I remember running around some chairs in our gym class, and I had the fastest time in the whole school. That was pretty good, and I could really hold my head up high.

"In junior high and high school, I got more involved in sports," Jenner says. "The competition helped my reading problem as I gained more faith in myself. Of all the things I did as a young kid, involvement in sports had the greatest impact on my life.

"Other than the dyslexia, I was no different than anyone else as a youngster. We had no organized baseball; I didn't train for anything. We just played and had fun.

"I didn't have the kind of dad who was out there every weekend throwing the baseball, running with me or pushing. Most of my work, I did on my own. But my parents were interested in what I was doing. They didn't neglect me; they were always at the games."

Jenner adds, "There was a lot of self-motivation, because I could stand next to the guy who was a good reader and getting A's, and beat him playing football."

In junior high school, Jenner went out for wrestling, but developed a serious knee problem. "I really didn't get started in sports until basketball season, my freshman year at Sleepy Hollow High School," he says.

"During the summer, I did competitive water-skiing, I was always competing. In high school, I competed in football, basketball and track. My senior year, I was 6'1" and weighed 175 pounds.

"I graduated from Newton High School in Connecticut. The school wasn't doing too well athletically, and my grades were marginal. It didn't seem likely that I'd be picked up by any college, with that background.

"Through a friend of a friend, I was recruited by Graceland College in Lamoni, Iowa, to play football. After three weeks on the team, I had to have knee surgery, and decided at that point that I had better get out of that sport. The rest of my time there I focused on track and field.

"I ran my first decathlon in 1970 as a sophomore at Graceland. The first time I did it, I told myself 'If anything has my name on it, this is it.'"

L. D. "Jack" Weldon, Jenner's track coach at Graceland, was himself a world-class javelin thrower. He recognized Jenner's athletic potential and encouraged him to train for the Olympic Decathlon.

"It was great," Jenner remembers, "because I could see so many areas for improvement. The decathlon was by far the most challenging thing I had found. I'd always done many kinds of sports, and here was an opportunity to combine all these activities into one sport. I began to concentrate on the decathlon. I wanted to know how good I could be at something.

"In 1971 I trained relatively hard, and there were some big improvements. In 1972, I was coming along well enough and thought I might make the qualifying standards for the Olympic Games. That year I did nothing but train for the trials. To qualify, I needed 7600 points. In the first meet I scored 7678 and qualified for the trials, which were held that year in Eugene, Oregon.

"At this point I was hoping to make the team. By the skin of my teeth and to my amazement, I did make the team. This was probably the biggest athletic thrill I had ever had in my life," he says. "I didn't really expect it. I was just hoping.

"During the 1500 meters, the last event, I had to have a good race. I needed to win by 18 seconds over one of the competitors. I ran eight seconds faster than I had ever done before and won by 21 seconds.

"All through the training, all the athletes pretty much coached each other. I knew what had to be done and was terribly motivated. There were a great group of athletes in the San Jose area—world class shot-putters, discus throwers, vaulters, sprinters and hurdlers, you name it—they were all within a five-mile radius of the house. I could get the best coaching in the world, because I could train with the guys who were competing.

"For example," Jenner says, "I could throw the discus with Mac Wilkins and John Powell."

Wilkins held the American discus throwing record five times, the world record four times, was a member of four Olympic teams, and won the gold in 1976. He was also nationally ranked in the shot put and hammer throw. Powell made four Olympic teams, and was six-time national champion in the discus throw.

"The first day at San Jose," he continues, "I was in the weight room with Maren Seidler. She outlifted me!"

Seidler was the premier American women's shot putter for 13 years. She won 23 national titles, was ranked first in America 11 times, made four Olympic teams, and was a member of 20 international teams.

"Suddenly, my perception of what was good changed drastically. I went from not being ranked in the top ten in the world to being number one the following year.

"The change in training had a big impact on me. I had the opportunity to train with these athletes, and I wasn't a threat to them. All of them took it upon themselves to make sure their specialty was working for me. All of them were helpful and wanted to see me do well.

"At the 1972 Games in Munich no one expected me to do much, so there was little pressure. While I was there, I learned as much as I could and saw Nikolai Avilov (USSR) get the gold medal (Avilov would finish with the bronze in 1976). I said to myself, 'This is what I'm going to do for the next four years.' I trained one more year in Iowa, and then moved to California to train in the San Jose area." During the training in San Jose, one piece of furniture in his living room was a high hurdle.

"When I entered the 1976 Games in Montreal, I had the world's record, and had lost only one meet during the last three years of my career. I'd done my homework and was physically and mentally ready. The pressure was on, because in 1972 no one had cared what I did. But in 1976, the world was watching and I went in with a tremendous amount of pressure both from myself and others.

"Every breath was crucial," Jenner remembers, "but I was so ready for the competition that I was able to come through, performance after performance. In the first event, the 100 meters, I ran the fastest electronic time I had ever run—10.94. For me, this was really good because I didn't have much speed. I was ecstatic with that time—it was better than I expected. It was my best time, and no one else had bettered theirs.

"Getting ready for the final event, the 1500-meter race, I knew I had won the meet already—I could feel it. All I had to do was run the 1500 in whatever time—I was going to win. I thought to myself then—the rest of my life is going to be easy, because I'd learned so much right there.

"The life of a truly dedicated athlete is not what I consider a well-rounded life. It's great to score points, but you have to invest a great deal and give up so much—family, friends, outings, having fun—those kinds of things.

"I didn't miss them at the time, because I wanted to do exactly what I was doing, and that was training and working for more and more points. I worked seven days a week, 365 days a year, because I was so totally into it, in every way.

"Now that I look back on it," Jenner says, "those four years between 1972 and 1976 were pretty dull. All I did was train. That was it; it was my whole life. There are no business opportunities, nothing on the outside.

But what you get from going through it all is a chance to learn so much about yourself. You can take all this knowledge and it will last you a lifetime. You realize what it takes to get ahead in whatever you are doing: You put your nose to the grindstone, and if you are going to fall, you are going to go flat on your face.

"When I was training, running and competing, I learned from each experience. I beat my head against the wall until it worked right. It's the same philosophy in the business world or in raising a child. You are constantly reminded that to get ahead, you have to work at it.

"I have never run since the last day of the Games. I knew going in that it would be the last time I would compete. On July 30, 1976, it would be all over—win, lose or draw. It was a big card to play, and it was hard, because it was sad. Here I was at the peak of my career. I beat the rest of the world, sang my greatest song, and will never sing again.

"Entertainers don't do that," he says, "actors don't. No matter what it is, if they have a talent they continue on with that talent. For me, using that talent was over.

"I cried my eyes out the last day of the Games. My whole life was wrapped up. The positive side was that I knew there was finality to the event. I could give up my job and start to raise a family. There were plenty of things I wanted to do with my life other than just concentrating on this.

"I didn't mind giving up my job and all the rest; I knew I could pick up those pieces. In that way, it gave me a great singleness of purpose. I knew exactly what I wanted to do and could do it without worrying about anything else. So at 7 P.M. on July 30, I started picking up the pieces."

Jenner says that going into the work world initially posed no fear for him. Coming out of his win at the Games, he found that people were offering him jobs. He says, "This was a very nice position to be in. The biggest problem I had was my own insecurities. Suddenly, I was asked to do something that others had more experience with, and because I was dyslexic I lacked intellectual confidence.

"It never occurred to me that someone would keep me around just because I was Bruce Jenner. I was willing to spend the extra time learning about business, and worked just a little harder to get the job done right. I always felt like I put a lot of pressure on myself to do things well, to make friends with my co-workers. I tried to always show up on time, know my lines and marks, and get it right the first time, because that guy running the camera wanted to go home just as much as I did.

"I took my work seriously and humbly. At first I didn't have much confidence in some of the work areas, especially with teleprompters. They would scare anyone, let alone someone who has a dyslectic problem. But now, some of my biggest thrills are going out on a live show in front of millions of people. Doing that has given me a lot of confidence through the years.

"As in all sports, we have to acknowledge that there is a great drug problem in track. My personal view is that you don't need drugs. I never took anything and made it all the way through. It's definitely a moral issue—using drugs to get up for games and down—all that stuff. It's so wrong, and it can kill you.

"I have had such tremendous highs in my life—the highs from competition were particularly great. I enjoyed the rush I got from competing. I race cars now. I sit in a car, get ready to race, and know I am alive. I can feel my heart pump and the adrenaline going, and I say 'I'm ready and here.' This is what life is all about. To the young people coming up, I would say 'Never ever underestimate the potential that lies inside of you.'

"Never in my wildest dreams in junior high, high school, or even college, did I think I would go out and become the best in the world at something. I thought those kinds of things happened to other guys, but not to me.

"I'm no different than anyone else—no superhuman being. Sometimes people look at you differently because of what you've accomplished, but I'm no different than they are. I was very fortunate in one area of my life and worked hard to realize that potential. This doesn't mean that the rest of your life is perfect, or that you deserve to be put on a pedestal. I feel very fortunate to have been able to go through an experience like the decathlon. It really enriched my life, and not just financially.

"When I look at my kids, the one thing I want to teach them is to find some area in their life—baseball, art, music, relationships with their family—and 'take it to the max,' as we say in California. I want them to see how far they can go, how much they can learn—in school or in whatever they are doing."

Jenner believes that the work and ideas developed in one area of life can be put into other areas. "The same work ethic and attitudes you find in sports will help you in business," he says. "There are thousands of things you can do in this world." Jenner is frequently quoted as saying that success "is not measured by heights obtained, but by obstacles overcome."

"When I was training," he says, "I used to think that everyone else was getting ahead of me in business, marriage, family—all those things that I wanted in my life. But, in a way, I knew I was richer because I had a tremendous purpose in life, and this discipline would eventually move me on to other goals."

Still physically active, Jenner rides mountain bikes, golfs, flies his own jet, and races cars professionally in Grand Prix events.

Jenner has ten children and has been named Parent of the Year by several prominent organizations. When asked how he wants to be remembered, Jenner says "as a good parent." He encourages his children "to find something in life to get excited about when they wake up in the morning." He is an avid supporter of Athletes and Entertainers for Kids. He has also been a member of the board of COACH for Kids, a program that provides health care to underprivileged children in the Los Angeles area. Both he and his wife serve, too, on the board of The Dream Foundation, which grants wishes to terminally ill adults.

Jenner presents motivational speeches on a regular basis to such companies as: IBM Corporation, Chrysler, Toyota, Kawasaki, Maytag, VISA, Coca Cola, Mack Trucks and Anheuser Busch. He turned down the title role in *Superman*, and was featured in Parker Brothers' "Bruce Jenner Board Game." Interactive Magic developed the computer game "Bruce Jenner's World Class Decathlon." The Franklin Mint featured a Bruce Jenner collectible ring. Jenner was also featured on the front of the Wheaties box for seven years, and later returned to the spot along with other superstar athletes including Tiger Woods and Michael Jordan.

6

Payton "Payt" Jordan

OLYMPIC COACH
Born March 19, 1917, Whittier, California

Payton Jordan was an all-around athlete at the University of Southern California, where he played football and rugby. As a member of the USC track team, he helped set the world's record in the 4 × 110-yard relay. Jordan was a member of two NCAA championship teams and was captain of the winning team his senior year (1939). In 1941, he won the 110-meter sprint for the AAU championship.

Jordan began his coaching career at Occidental College and helped move their track and field team into national prominence, with ten consecutive league championships and an NAIA (National Association of Intercollegiate Athletics) national title. His distance relay team set a world record, and individual athletes won four NCAA championships. Occidental running star Bob McMillen won the silver in the 1500 meters at the 1952 Olympic Games in Helsinki.

Jordan also coached the freshman football team at Occidental to five conference titles and a tie for the sixth. Included in his team line-up were Jack Kemp, (1957) future pro-quarterback, U.S. Senator and presidential candidate, and Jim Mora (1957), assistant football coach at Stanford, coach of the Indianapolis Colts, and the New Orleans Saints.

Jordan moved to Stanford University in 1957, and over the course of the next 23 years, he coached seven Olympians, six national champions and six world record holders. He was instrumental in bringing the 1960 Olympic trials to Stanford, was assistant track coach for the 1964 Games in Tokyo and head coach of the 1968 U.S. Olympic Track Team in Mexico City.

Jordan continued his athletic career as a sprinter in the Masters

Payton Jordan (coach). (Courtesy Payton Jordan.)

competitions, setting American and World records in age groups from 55 to 80 in the 100-meter and 200-meter sprints.

Career Achievements

- Payton Jordan was elected to the Helms Athletic Foundation Track and Field Hall of Fame in 1970.

- He was inducted into the National Track and Field Hall of Fame in 1982.

- A strong supporter of the Mt. SAC (San Antonio College) Relays, Jordan was inducted as a coach into the Mt. SAC Hall of Fame in 1983. Membership honors coaches and athletes who have made "significant contributions to the Relays and the sport of track and field."

- Jordan was inducted into the Occidental Hall of Fame in 1985 and the Stanford Hall of Fame in 1991.

- He was inducted into the United States Track Coaches Association National Hall of Fame in 1997.

- Jordan was inducted into the NAIA (National Association of Intercollegiate Athletics) Hall of Fame in 1992 and the Senior Athletes Hall of Fame that same year.

- He was inducted into the USA Track and Field Masters Hall of Fame and won the Arete Award for Pursuit of Excellence and Courage in Sports in 1997.

- The U.S. Sports Academy honored Jordan with the Dwight D. Eisenhower Fitness Award in 1999.

- Jordan was named Track and Field Coach, Emeritus at Stanford University in 1980, and awarded the degree of Doctor of Humane Letters by Occidental College in 2001.

- When Jordan directed the USA/USSR dual track meet, more than 15,000 people turned out for the event, one of the most popular in track history.

- Jordan's 1968 Olympic Track team won more medals and set more records than any other U.S. Team.

- Jordan is the author, with Bud Spencer, of *Champions in the Making; Quality Training for Track and Field*.

- *Champions for Life*, by John B. Scott and James S. Ward chronicles Jordon's influence on the athletes he has worked with.

- In 1941, Jordan ran 9.5 in the 100-yard dash and set the world's record for a grass track that lasted for 27 years. (Jordan ran an unofficial 9.3 in the 100-yard dash in 1939, when the world's record was 9.4.)

Tips from the Coach

Jordan believes that all athletes can add to their competitive edge with a program to increase speed. According to Jordan, there are three ways to reach full speed potential: by increasing *strength, reaction* and *stride length.*

Strength can be increased by completing a weight program three times a week. For maximum results, he suggests beginning each session with stretching and loosening calisthenics, followed by running. The weight exercises he suggests are goose stepping, while carrying 35 percent of body weight on the shoulders (barbell, weight vest); half squats with 50–75 percent of body weight, using a barbell; leg lifts on an incline board; and in-place knee lifts with 3–5 pound iron boots.

To increase reaction time, Jordan suggests egg-shell running (fast in-place running). He believes that if you want to run faster, the first step is to move faster. He also recommends high knee lifting and vigorous arm swings, to develop a more efficient movement pattern.

To extend stride length, Jordan recommends hip-swing and a full arm swing drill, and a power-drive that vigorously moves the leg through the full range of motion. Running forward on the toes, exaggerating the knee lift and keeping both shoulders and jaw loose all help develop stride length.

Interview

> "We are so lucky ... as we nurture these young champions; perhaps in some way we ennoble and enrich those people who watch them compete."—Payton Jordan, speaking to a group of U.S. Olympic Track and Field Coaches

Interviewer's Notes

A poster that hung in Jordan's office asked: "Is it safe? Is it popular? Is it politic? Is it right?" Jordan said that the only one that mattered was the last question. "If it's right, I'll do it. If it's not, I won't."

I first met Payton Jordan at the NAIA Championships in Sioux Falls, South Dakota. Later on, when he was head coach for the 1968 Olympics, we met and talked at Lake Tahoe. He was always kind and patient, and seemed not be be bothered by endless questions and comments. He was youthful in his appearance, and in his 70s gave younger runners fits in the 100-meter run. He was a keen student of track and field and was always receptive to anyone who wanted to talk about the sport.

* * * * *

When Jordan was asked about the first time he knew there was such a thing as sport, he replied that he was quite active as a young boy. "When I was seven or eight," he remembers, "there was a retired ship captain, a Mr. Nash, who lived in our area. He encouraged us to do things that would keep us out of mischief. He taught us how to build boats and encouraged us to race each other in the hilltop area of Sierra Madre. This was the beginning of my desire to compete—low key, but a beginning.

"We also had a horse stable up in the mountains behind our house— the Quorum Stables. The cowboys there teased us by having us run and then trying to rope us. I could run a little faster than some of the kids, so they had trouble roping me. It was like running for your life," he remembers.

"At Sierra Madre Grammar School we had the usual physical education activities, but at the junior high level there were more formal competitions. There were four junior high schools in Pasadena, a city wide open with opportunities to compete in various athletic events.

"I loved all kinds of sports, but I think my favorite has always been track and field. Both my mother and father were very athletic," Jordan says. "My father was an outstanding high school athlete. He played on the California High School Championship football team. He was also an excellent track man, baseball player and amateur boxer.

"My mother was equally athletic. Although sports for women were not in vogue at that time, she could run faster than most of the other girls.

"So I had a good gene pool," he says, "and God blessed me. It goes without saying that my parents were very supportive—always behind me and helping me to realize what I could do in sports, as well as in academics.

"My teachers and early coaches were equally interested in each of us and gave us good guidance," Jordan adds. "It was fun for me to test myself with my friends. When we competed, I would usually be in the top 10 percent. I had a great childhood—living in the open country and having the opportunity to do many things.

"When I entered high school," Jordan says, "my interests, other than sports, were in history and art. I loved music, but I wasn't particularly good at it. I did have a saxophone, and played loudly, but not with much expertise.

"My folks encouraged me to do as well as possible in school, but I usually put more emphasis on sports than academics. In high school, my teachers became more important to me, and they encouraged me to go on to college. It stuck in my mind that if I had goals and ambitions, they would have a way of coming true.

"I followed the University of Southern California, because they were big in the Los Angeles area, and Dean Cromwell was big in track and field. I thought Cromwell was a terrific coach, and began to think that coaching might be of interest to me.

"I went to the Olympics in Los Angeles with my mother in 1932. We were sitting in the Coliseum watching Eddie Tolan and Ralph Metcalfe run the 200-meter race, and I turned to my mother and said 'I sure want to do something like that when I get bigger.' I told her that I wanted to go to USC, where Cromwell coached.

"I thought it would be fun to be a coach," Jordan says. "I started dreaming about this at the age of 13 or 14, and had some goals, but they weren't solid. When I got to college, all those thoughts became important to me.

"Growing up during the Depression, my financial situation was rather bleak. My folks had very little money, and keeping a job was a problem. We lived frugally, but pretty well, because we were out in the country and could raise things to eat. Sometimes, I think it was a blessing, because we didn't eat junk food. We ate simple foods and lived simply, and the result was that we got stronger and better.

"As a kid," Jordan remembers, "I worked at whatever I could do—making a nickel here or there. I had a milk route in the morning and after school I worked at Roberts Market. It was roustabout work and provided a wonderful opportunity to get some food. In the evenings, I had a paper route.

"Once a week, I had the opportunity to work at the swimming pool. I was paid a dollar and a half for cleaning the pool, which required four or five hours of scrubbing. All this gave me a little money and helped augment some of the needs at home.

"One of my idols at that time was Charlie Paddock, a Pasadena native, who was rated the world's fastest runner."

In the early 1920s, Paddock held five National AAU sprint titles and was the first to run the 200 in less than 21 seconds. He served in World War I, and after the war, won the 100 and 200-meter races at the 1919 Inter-Allied Games, where soldiers of the Allied nations competed against each other. In 1920, he won the silver in the 200-meter, and gold medals for the 100-meter dash and the 4 × 100 relay team, which included U.S. teammates **Jackson Scholz,** Morris Kirksey and Loren Murchison.

Paddock earned a silver in the 200 at the 1924 Olympics, and made the 1928 team, but failed to qualify for the 200-meter final. His trademark finishing style was a leap toward the line, at the end of a race. Paddock ran the 110-yard race in 10.2 seconds, a record that wasn't broken until 1956. Jordan's chances to participate in the Olympic Games were curtailed by the cancellation of the games in 1940 and 1944, during World War II. After World War I and during World War II, Paddock was on the staff of Major General William Upshur. Both Paddock and Upshur were killed in a plane crash near Sitka, Alaska, in 1943.

Jordan continues, "Paddock was finished with his running career and was working for the *Pasadena Star News* as a sports writer. He did a column called 'Stars in the Making.' I'd run in a junior high meet and had a fairly good day. He came up to me, hit me in the shoulder and said, 'Son, you keep working, and someday you will be a champion.'

"If you think I didn't get excited!" Jordan says. "I went home and told my mom and dad; I was so thrilled, I just couldn't believe it.

"During my high school years, recruiting wasn't a big thing," Jordan remembers. "Nobody threw money in your face. You just gravitated to the school you liked. We considered it a great honor just to talk to the coaches of the schools. We felt it was an opportunity to go to college, take part in their sports and get the education available to us.

"There were nine us who ended up going to USC," he adds. "It was quite a group—all of us from Pasadena High School. Our high school— and even junior high teams—were very close knit groups. We all had great respect for each other and loved to compete. We were really thrilled to be part of team competition, in any sport.

"With close friendships like these, there are many stories which we shared. Louie Zamperini, National Champion miler, was one of the great war heroes. He was shot down in the South Pacific and drifted with his fellow pilots and airmen for 47 days, until he was picked up by the Japanese. He was treated brutally and taken to Japan. The story is of epic proportions—the book and movie of this adventure (*Devil at My Heels*) are fascinating.

"Clark Mallory, our high jumper, won the IC4A Championships

(Intercollegiate Association of Amateur Athletes of America) and became a great cartoonist for the Disney corporation. He later organized the famous *Five Plus Three* jazz band.

"Mike Portenova, the great distance runner and steeple chaser, was head manager for the 1968 Olympic team, the year I was head track coach. Mike and I went to high school, college and club athletics together and then we both became involved in the 1968 Olympics.

"All the other fellows have equally interesting stories," Jordan says. "We've had fun together and shared a lot of great times." (Later, Michael Portanova [2-miler] and Payton Jordan [sprints], classmates at Pasadena High School and USC, were named head manager and head track coach, respectively, of the 1968 Olympic track team—the first two from the same school ever to be so honored.)

When Jordan was captain of the University of Southern California national championship track and field team, he was on the cover of *Life* magazine with the caption "Captain of Champions." The description of the *Life* cover read: "The sprinter is 21-year-old Payton Jordan, who lives in Pasadena and has a scholarship at the University of Southern California. Jordan is captain of America's Greatest Track Team, which won the Intercollegiate Association of Amateur Athletes of America [competition] in New York last month, hands down" (*Life* Magazine, June 19, 1939).

Asked to comment on the place of role models in athletics, Jordan says, "A role model is someone who stands out, above and beyond everyone else. The important thing is what he is or becomes, not what he says.

"I've already cited the name of Charlie Paddock, who was an important role model for me in the early stages of my development. I also credit my wonderful coach, Dean Cromwell at USC. I would have to say that my high school coach, Carl Mentten, had a tremendous influence on helping me set goals and guiding me toward my education, athletics and a coaching career. Those three people stand out as unique and special role models.

"When retirement came along," Jordan says" I had planned ahead. I thought that after 40 years of coaching, I might step aside and find some other interests and spend more time with my family, grandkids and great-grandkids—and to smell the roses for a while.

"I didn't retire because I was tired; I just felt it was the time. It gave me the opportunity to explore other interests and do other things. I actually got back into Masters track. I met old friends and new challenges. There was excitement! It was a good carryover from active coaching—a return to kid-like activities," he says.

Commenting on the encroachment of professionalism into athletics, Jordan says, "I watched professionalism enter into our sport, and I believe it has possibly been abused. I'm a purist, I guess. I can accept reasonable financial rewards for taking part in the marathons, but when they are excessive and the athletes become greedy, I have reservations. I also worry about drugs in our sport," he says. "Drugs are just not worth it."

Asked what influence athletics have had in his life, Jordan replies, "Health-wise, sports are the atmosphere in which you can function and realize the best of all worlds. You are outdoors and dealing with people who are motivated. You are exercising and stimulated by the efforts of others. It's an exciting and emotional activity.

"Lots of problems pop up in life that need to be solved, and you learn to take charge. Leadership is most effective when it is done by example. You work at developing a value system, where people realize they have to be committed. It takes discipline, if you are going to be successful.

"If you lack discipline," Jordan adds, "this is where the coach steps in. I emphasized goals. Dreams and goals are part of being successful, as well as faith and belief—the ability to say 'thank you' and show appreciation to other people who have helped you along the way.

"Out of this comes wonderful friendships—with our fellow coaches, athletes and fans that follow your sport and believe that what you're doing is worthwhile."

Asked where we are heading with sports, Jordan replies that key decision points in the future will deal with professionalism and the use of drugs to enhance performance. "Sports are still a wonderful part of our society," he says. "They bring so much value to our way of living, and create a great interest in all areas of life.

Does it matter whether you win or lose? Jordan is asked.

"Anything you attempt should be done as well as you can do it," he says. "If you are the best you can be, then you are a winner. One must also learn to accept defeat and understand it is not the end of the world."

When asked to talk about his honors and awards, Jordan says, "There have been so many magnificent things that have happened in my life, but I think the most important are the friendships and memories of all the wonderful people I've met.

"One particular honor is when someone names a child after me. Seventeen athletes and coaches have been so kind as to think my name was worthy of being given to their children. I think this might be the biggest award a person can have. You know, in coaching, you don't take a lot of money to the bank, but the relationships you have with your athletes certainly go to your heart." Jordan is currently the oldest Olympic coach.

7

Abel R. Kiviat

MIDDLE DISTANCES • SILVER MEDAL
Born June 23, 1892, New York, New York
Died August 24, 1991

Abel Kiviat, considered to be one of the world's greatest middle distance runners, was the only runner in history to simultaneously hold the AAU indoor records for the 600-yard, 1000-yard and the mile distances. In 1911 he was one of the best runners in the country, becoming the first to win both the 600- and 1000-yard events. In 1913 he would repeat this performance, winning both on the same night. He was also a world record holder in outdoor track.

The 20-year-old Kiviat won a gold medal at the Stockholm Olympics as a member of the five-man 3,000-meter relay team. He set a world record of 3.55.8 in the 1500 meter run at the Olympic trials (called "the greatest race ever run" by sports writer Cordner Nelson), and was expected to win the gold medal.

In the lead with just 50 meters to go, Kiviat was outdistanced by British runner Arnold Jackson, who finished first in 3:56.8. Kiviat and his fellow American runner, Norman Tabor, both finished at 3.56.9. In what was to be the first "photo finish" in history, the silver medal was awarded to Kiviat. Despite his loss at the Olympics, Kiviat's personal best record of 3:55.8 in the 1500-meter race remained the world's record until 1917.

After serving in France during World War I, Kiviat competed in events until 1925. He maintained a lifelong interest in track, serving as a press steward at major meets. He carried the Olympic torch for the opening ceremony of the Games in 1986.

Career Achievements

- While he was still a high school student, Kiviat won five national indoor titles and four outdoor titles: three in the mile and one in cross country. He won three National AAU titles and ran a 4.23 mile. Sports historians believe that if his lack of training, poor quality of running shoes, and slow cinder tracks were factored into his achievements, Kiviat's time would come closer to a four-minute mile.

- Kiviat was named to the Public Schools Athletic League team as shortstop the same night that he broke PSAL records in the half mile and the mile.

- Kiviat won the New York Athletic Club Games Baxter Mile, the most important mile event in America at that time.

- He was the winner of the American Six-Mile Cross Country title.

- He established a U.S. Indoor Mile record of 4:18.2.

- He competed in the Canadian National Championship races, and broke his first world record in the two-thirds mile at 2:47.2.

- He beat the world 1500-meter record three times. His final time of 3:55.8 lasted for five years.

- In 1985, Kiviat was inducted into the Track and Field Hall of Fame and the International Jewish Sports Hall of Fame.

- When he was in high school, Kiviat was asked to join the famed Irish-American Athletic Club. He became its most famous member and served as captain of the track team for five years.

- *Runners World* listed Kiviat's times among the best performances for the 1500 meters, including a 3:59.2 in New York on May 26, 1912; a 3:56.8 at the same venue on June 2, and a 3:55.8 six days later in Cambridge, Mass.

Interview

"Do you know who handed me the torch? It was Jim Thorpe's grandson and Jesse Owens' granddaughter, who ran together as one."

Abel Kiviat (middle distances, first on left). (Courtesy the United States Track and Field Library.)

Interviewer's Notes

Abel Kiviat was in his 90s when I interviewed him at his home in Lakehurst, New Jersey. He recalled clearly and in detail the events of his early years in athletics, and the two hours spent on his back porch were a fascinating trip to the past.

Through our conversation, I was taken back to the turn of the twentieth century, when the modern Olympics had just begun. The great athletes of those days—Jim Thorpe (Kiviat's roommate at the Olympics), Tommy Knitt, Oscar Hedlund, Jack Kelley and Johnny Hayes—were competitors and friends, and all were gone.

Abel spoke at length about his friendship with Jim Thorpe, and was proud to have been on the same team with him. But it noticeably bothered him to tell about Jim being so poor that he didn't have a Waterman (pen) to sign his own autograph.

* * * * *

"I was born in 1892," Kiviat said, by way of introduction. "My folks ran a general store and sold a little of everything. There were six boys and one girl in our family, and all us boys were athletes. As kids in the country we played all kinds of games, so we were really running all the time."

Kiviat remembers that they could buy a baseball for ten cents, but it would last only a day. "If you wanted to use it again, you bought a roll of black tape for five cents and taped it back together. And if you didn't have a glove on, it would murder your fingers," Kiviat says.

He also remembers running for medals once a year in grammar school. "The race was on hard brick, right in front of the school," he says, "and we had to run 100 yards in 15 seconds to qualify. There were no track suits, just civilian clothes, and the teacher had to borrow a stop watch."

Kiviat qualified under 15 seconds for the races in 1903, '04, and '05, and won the half-bronze, half-silver medals all three years.

"I knew I was pretty fast," Abel notes, "because when I played baseball I could steal more bases on the grammar school baseball team than anyone else. I was captain of that team. Later, I went to Curtis High School and went out for football. I weighed about 102 pounds and was five feet tall. I played as a wide end, about the time the forward pass came out in 1907."

In high school, Kiviat made the all-scholastic baseball and track team, but he reports that playing football nearly killed him. "I was laid up for seven weeks with a broken collarbone, walking around with my elbow and arm sticking out."

He tried football again, but broke his nose. "My folks, being European people, asked me, 'Is this what we send you to an American high school for?'"

So how did one of the fastest middle distance runners get his start?

"When April came around," Kiviat says, "I went out for baseball. The track surrounded our baseball and football field. In those days it was the only place where we had a track. Other schools from lower Manhattan were allowed to use the facilities, so we usually practiced until they got there.

"One day, a track team was working out and a good friend of mine, who was captain of the track team, said, 'Come on out. I've got donations for a bronze medal that costs $1.25. I'll give everybody a 50-yard head start.'

"So the baseball gang all gave it a try. One of them was Elroy Ripley, later the famous coach of basketball at Notre Dame, Yale and West Point. At the time, he was the first baseman and catcher on our team. He ran and so did I, both of us in baseball uniforms and a pair of cheap spikes."

Kiviat won the race with the 50-yard handicap, and joined the track team. "We all got together," Kiviat says, "the baseball captain and manager, the track captain and manager—and arranged things so both teams could work out the same days. When we went to Brooklyn or the Bronx we made the same arrangement, so I would run the same day we played baseball."

By the end of June the baseball team had won the championship, and the coaches convinced Kiviat to run the half mile and the mile in track competition. "I ran away with the mile in 4.40.8," Kiviat says. It was the new high school record for New York.

The race Kiviat never forgot was the half mile where he met the previous year's champion of 1907-8, Cedric Major from Brooklyn. "We ran the half mile in almost a dead heat in 2.04.4," he says. "I won that one, and it was a school record."

Robin Edwin, famous cartoonist and sports editor of the *New York Evening World*, showed up at the track the day Kiviat won the half mile. Edwin showed Kiviat several cartoons he had drawn, which appeared in the paper.

"In those days," Kiviat reports, "we wore knickerbocker pants (knee-pants), long socks, and garters to play baseball. He drew me dressed up like that and called me the 'Jewish Hans Wagner.'" (Legendary shortstop and batter, John Peter "Honus" or "Hans" Wagner, played for the Kentucky Colonels and the Pittsburgh Pirates. He was one of the first inductees into the Baseball Hall of Fame in 1936, and the first to have his signature embedded in a Louisville slugger bat.)

Lawson Robertson—Olympic medalist (standing high jump, standing long jump), Olympic track coach for many years, and coach of the famous Irish American Athletic Club—was an official the day of the Championships. Kiviat remembers that, after the races, Robertson invited him to join the Irish American Club. (Robertson was to be Kiviat's only coach.) The Irish Athletic Club was commonly known as the "Poor Man's Club."

"The wealthier boys joined the New York Athletic Club," Kiviat says. "We wore the winged fist on Irish green and they wore the New York Athletic Club winged foot," he says. "There was always great competition between the two clubs."

At that time, Celtic Park was a nine-acre athletic field on Long Island, bordering Queens. "There were bleachers set up, and for a quarter you could see a big track meet," Kiviat says. "Before a meet, there would be half a dozen Irish fiddlers playing in a big social area outdoors, while their wives and daughters took up a collection.

"When the Irish athletes came in from Ireland, they joined the Irish American Club because they felt at home." Kiviat says. He notes that he was the only Jew in the club, and they made him captain of the track club. In return, he did small favors for his fellow club members.

"For instance, there was a big Catholic Church, and on Sundays the athletes went through a private gate to go to church. I got them coffee to keep them awake during the service, and fresh milk from next door, where there was a little farm."

The Irish American Athletic Club was formed in 1897 to promote participation in a variety of games: track and field, Irish football, hurling, bicycling and handball. The club was a training ground for many champions and record holders. At the 1908 Games in London, eight of the thirteen U.S. medalists in track and field were members of the Irish American Athletic Club.

In 1908, Kiviat began reading about track and field. "When Mel Sheppard won the half mile and the mile, this made big headlines, even in the local papers on Staten Island. People started kidding me," Kiviat says, "asking me why I didn't go into track."

"Peerless" Mel Sheppard was the first person to win gold medals in both the 800 and 1500-meter races, setting world records in each at the 1908 London Olympic Games. He also held seven national AAU middle distance championships, and medaled for the gold on the 1908 medley relay and the 1912 4 × 400 relay.

"Well, I stuck it out," Kiviat says, "and in 1908 and 1909 I became famous by winning the mile and the half-mile championships. In those days, track athletes were not allowed to run on the roads. We did most of our training on the track."

The first job Kiviat had after high school was in 1909, when he went to work for Wanamaker's Department Store (one of the first and most famous American department stores, now Lord and Taylor). He was a salesman in the sporting goods department, earning $15 a week. He worked from 8 A.M. to 6 P.M., and during December he worked until midnight. His commute home took two hours.

"I ran relays for Wanamaker's in the industrial league," Kiviat says. "Macy's and Gimbel Brothers were about ready to come into the picture, but Wanamaker had the most athletes."

At the end of the 19th century and the beginning of the 20th, participation in athletic clubs was often restricted to those who belonged to the wealthiest class. Industrial leagues opened participation in competitive sports to those who could not afford memberships in the elite clubs. Many businesses promoted themselves by actively recruiting the best unaffiliated athletes to work for them and participate in competitive meets.

Wanamaker's encouraged Kiviat to join the 13th Regiment of the National Guard, so he also ran on the Guard team. They ran at Madison

Square Garden, which was abandoned at the time, and the 13th Regiment had the best track team.

"I kept up my running with Wanamaker's and the National Guard until World War I came along," Kiviat says. "I volunteered. I didn't stop to think what I was doing, except—all right, they could count on me. In April, we were federalized and sailed for Europe.

"My wife didn't like it," Kiviat remembers, "and I had a son who was then three years old."

But Kiviat proudly adds that his son grew up to make the military his career, and eventually retired as an Army colonel.

Kiviat missed holding the outdoor mile record by one-fifth of a second, but held the world indoor record for years.

He also held the indoor records for the 600-yard and 1000-yard runs. Kiviat says, "I did something that had not been done before or since. Of all the athletes that competed, I was the only athlete to run both, and I was a double winner. In 1913, I repeated that and made a World's Record."

Kiviat ran in Yankee Stadium, at the Polo Grounds, and the AAU track meets at the old Ebbets Field in Brooklyn. He reports that it was easier for him to run indoors than out.

"The track measured in 18 inches from the border, and being a shrimp, I could run inside the 18 inches. I wasn't cheating because that was permitted. I could beat the bigger fellows with their 11- and 12-foot strides. Here I was, 5'1", with a seven- or eight-foot stride, but I could hold the pole. They couldn't take the turns. They would go way out, and I could take them on the turns and gain 10 or 15 yards. It was the straightaways that gave me trouble.

"To get to the 1912 Olympics, you had to qualify in the finals at Harvard Stadium," Kiviat says. "The trial heats were held in Chicago, San Francisco, or Los Angeles. We had a semifinal meet in the Polo Grounds. The following week, the finals were held at Harvard.

"Three athletes were picked in each race. I was made a triple. They put me in the 800 meter, the 1500 meter and the 3000 meter. I only qualified in the 1500 meter. My best time for the indoor record was 4:18.1. The previous record was held by Oscar Hedlund, the New England AAU Champion, who later became head coach at MIT."

The team left New York for Stockholm in 1912, on board the S.S. *Finland,* of the old Red Star Line. "There were a few non-athletes aboard, who went first class paying full fare, which helped the athletes with their expenses," Kiviat says. "Most of the people aboard, however, were Olympic athletes, managers, and a couple of 'rubbers' or masseurs/trainers. They made a running area out of a board five or six feet wide that went around the ship. You couldn't really race, but you could pass each other."

The trip lasted ten days. Kiviat says that the *Titanic* had sunk in April, and between bouts of seasickness, the athletes stood on deck and looked for the iceberg that had sunk the *Titanic*.

"We landed in Europe in Rotterdam and went ashore there for a day. Mike Murphy was picked as Olympic Coach, and Lawson Robertson was his first assistant. Robertson had been on the 1904 (St. Louis) and 1908 (London) Olympic teams as a sprinter."

Michael Murphy (Track and Field Hall of Fame, Penn Hall of Fame, head track coach at Yale and Penn State) was considered a coaching innovator. He developed the crouch start for sprinters, and had ten National AAU team titles. In 1912, he was suffering from tuberculosis and other illnesses but coached the spring track season. In the fall, he collapsed while coaching football and died the following June. Murphy was the father of George Murphy, actor and U.S. senator.

Kiviat continues, "After Rotterdam, we landed in Hobachen, and there we were put on the S.S. *Olympic* to sail into the harbor in Stockholm. They had an area dredged so we could anchor against a stone dock. We lived on the ship, but to really train we had to go inland. They got us a small tug boat and a half dozen row boats that would hold eight or ten athletes, and towed us to the training area."

Kiviat remembers his most satisfying win to be the 1500-meter finals in Harvard Stadium, "when Norman Tabor chased me all the way, almost to the tape. His time was one-fifth of a second slower than mine. This occurred just a week before we sailed for Stockholm and the 1912 Olympics."

His biggest disappointment was his performance at the Olympics. "I was the favorite, and a lot of folks thought that race ended in a dead heat. Jackson [Arnold Jackson, Great Britain] was given the gold." (Jackson was clocked at 3:56.8, Kiviat at 3:56.9, and Norman Tabor at 3:56.9.)

"I did not use good judgment," Kiviat says. "It was about 120 yards short of a mile, or some 30 yards a lap short, so he jumped me going around the start of the last turn. As you come out of the turn it's a straightaway. When he jumped me, he got a five-yard lead before I woke up to the fact." When Kiviat lost the gold in Stockholm, he had not lost a race in two years.

Kiviat remembers that after the race the famous Arthur Daley, sports writer for the *New York Times*, asked him, "What were you waiting for, the Toonerville Trolley?" [This was a reference to a well-known cartoon drawn by Fontaine Fox, which depicted the adventures of an antiquated

electric car and its solicitous motorman.] "Daley's father was a great runner back in the 1880s and '90s," he adds.

The 1500-meter race in the 1912 Stockholm Games was named to
ESPN's Jeff Hollobaugh's list of "The [20th] Century's 100 Greatest
Competitions." To be considered for the list, a competition had to meet
the criteria of being both exciting and historically significant.

Kiviat was a great friend and admirer of Jim Thorpe, who was his
roommate at the Olympics. He remembers that Thorpe ran in the hurdles against Jack Kelley, the Olympic Champion. He also entered and
won two competitions new to the Olympics that year: the Pentathlon and
Decathlon. He won them both, Kiviat reports, through sheer natural skill
and strength. Thorpe had never thrown the discus or javelin but, in
unorthodox style, managed to win both events.

"Jim Thorpe was a great man," Kiviat says, "a perfectly quiet chap
who never had a penny to his name. He had nothing—not even a pen to
sign an autograph. Jim worked out mostly with the weight men, but I
didn't get to see him do much of that.

"I did get with him one time after the Olympic games. We went out
to play a baseball game. We were looking good in the fifth or sixth inning
when up comes Thorpe. He was in uniform and wanted to play with us,
the East team. He was feeling good and asked if he could have a ball. He
proceeded to throw it a mile over the left fielder's head. So we let him
play the last two or three innings."

Kiviat believes that today's athletes have distinct training advantages
over the athletes from his time. But the commitment to participate and
compete may have been stronger in his time.

"We didn't have full bed and expenses paid," he says. "It cost me 46
cents a day to get to Celtic Park, the training grounds for the Irish American Club outside Queens, Long Island. It was a long way to the grounds:
carfare from Staten Island, trolley cars, ferryboat, elevated to 34th Street,
shuttle to the waterfront, and a 3-cent ferryboat. Then a trolley car again
to Celtic Park and a quarter-mile walk to the entrance.

"We got no car fare and paid our own expenses. Some athletes in my
time received no help at all, but my club paid my expenses to go to Harvard for the final Olympic tryouts," Kiviat says, observing that "today an
athlete can't open his mouth without getting paid.

"You couldn't live at Celtic Park, but you could stay overnight and
maybe compete on Sunday. My folks showed some interest and didn't care
as long as nothing happened to me. Track wasn't like playing football
where I got a broken nose, collar bone, and shoulder blade," he laughs.

"With all I know today, I would do the same thing again," Kiviat says. "Athletics has given me a healthy life. I learned how to eat [Kiviat, like other runners of his generation, believed that a high protein diet, specifically meat, was essential for athletic performance. He claimed to dine often on rare roast beef], live right, and get plenty of sleep. I used to go to bed at 7 P.M. and I drank no liquor. I always had some sort of job after school—selling newspapers, running errands for a drug store, being a messenger boy, delivering medicine. So I sort of paid my own way.

"They ran a lot of professional marathons in Madison Square Garden," Kiviat notes. "Coaches in those days were conservative and did not want athletes to train every day.

"Lawson Robertson told me this: 'If you win three or four races in a row, you must have natural ability. Why in heaven do you have to train every day? You already have it!'

"One day, I would run for sprints or whatever, depending on the weakest part of my last race," Kiviat says. "If I let a fellow get too much of a lead in the middle of a race, then I would run two 600s at top pace. They would put a quarter miler against me to make me run.

"If I was almost beaten at the finish in handicapped races and I was out-sprinted, I would do two or three hundred-yard dashes. I practiced my starts, and if I could beat Halpern or Ted Meredith off the mark indoors, then I could grab the pole." (James "Ted" Meredith was a high school student when he won the Olympic gold in the 800 meters in Stockholm, and set a world record.)

When asked about his athletic performances, Kiviat believes he must have had some natural ability. "Otherwise I couldn't have won so many races, particularly the match races," he says. "I won the Baxter Cup five years in a row. Oscar Hedlund won it in the New York Athletic Club Games on a Saturday night; three days later I ran against the same gang, broke the World's Record, and won the mile special.

"That was on a flat floor, no spikes, at the 71st Regiment Armory. At Madison Square Garden, you could use spikes. In October of that year, I won the Senior National AAU Championship Cross Country Run at Van Courtland Park on a five-mile course."

Kiviat says that he has a collector's card with a picture of himself on the front, dressed in his track outfit. "A company got me to sign a release and gave me 25 dollars." Additional money was supposed to have come later, but the company used the picture and the money failed to materialize.

"In 1984, seventy-two years after the Olympics in Stockholm, my friend Bud Greenspan arranged for me to spend a week at the Grand Hotel. In 1912, the team was housed on the ship and we only got to *look* at the Grand Hotel! But this time, I was treated like a king. They paid all expenses. [Greenspan took nine athletes to Stockholm to film a documentary on the Olympics.]

During the carrying of the Olympic Torch in 1984, Kiviat represented New York City, sponsored by the New York Runners' Club. With pride he asks, "Do you know who handed me the torch? It was Jim Thorpe's grandson and Jesse Owen's granddaughter, who ran together as one."

Kiviat also remembers that "it was raining cats and dogs, and the wind was blowing. I was holding the torch up in front of me, extending my arm as high as I could. The uniforms were nothing like those in 1912. It felt like I was naked, running in that outfit!

"Staten Island used to be in the country. Now it's built up like any part of Manhattan and I don't even recognize it. I had a great time there as a kid. I go down to the family cemetery, and all the buildings are there. The cemetery is named after Baron Hirsch, a famous Jewish Revolutionary War general."

Kiviat was the only resident of Staten Island ever to compete in the Olympics. The Kiviat Track and Field Memorial event is held annually at Curtis High School on Staten Island.

The *Staten Island Advance* ranked Kiviat's Olympic win among the 100 most significant events in Staten Island history.

The Staten Island Athletic Club presents the Abel Kiviat Memorial Award to an outstanding runner each year.

The Abel R. Kiviat Memorial Track at Curtis High School is named for its famous graduate. The annual Vacation Run includes Abel R. Kiviat 1500-meter races for freshmen, sophomores and varsity.

The 1998 **Ken Doherty** Memorial Fellowship, established to promote research in the field of track and field, was awarded to Alan Katchen for his proposal "The Hebrew Runner: Abel Kiviat and His World."

Postscript

Abel Kiviat died in August 1991 at the age of 99. If he had lived, Kiviat would have carried the torch and lit the flame at the 1992 Olympics in Barcelona, Spain. At the time of his death, he was America's oldest Olympian.

8

Robert Bruce "Bob" Mathias

DECATHLON • TWO GOLD MEDALS
Born November 17, 1930, Tulare, California

In 1948, at the age of 17, Mathias was (and still is) the youngest member ever to compete with a United States Olympic track and field team. Outscoring Ignace Heinrich of France (silver) and his U.S. teammate Floyd Simmons (bronze), Mathias won the gold medal at the London games with a total of 7139 points, and became the youngest member of a U.S. track and field team to win the gold. He was also the only competitor to surpass 7000 points.

At the 1952 Games in Helsinki, Finland, Mathias broke his own world record, earning 7887 points and defeating U.S. teammate Milt Campbell by 912 points, the largest margin in Olympic history.

Mathias won three world decathlon competitions and set three world records. He was the U.S. national decathlon champion four times (1948, 1949, 1950, 1952), an unprecedented achievement. Mathias retired at age 21, undefeated.

Career Achievements

- Mathias was California Interscholastic Federation discus and shot put champion in 1947.

- When Mathias won the Olympic gold medal in 1948, he had competed in only two other decathlons.

Bob Mathias (decathlon). (Courtesy Stanford University.)

- He was the Associated Press Male Athlete of the Year in 1952.

- Mathias won the James E. Sullivan Memorial Award (presented annually by the AAU to the outstanding amateur athlete in the country).

- Mathias was inducted into the USA Track and Field Hall of Fame in 1974.

- He was a member of the first class inducted into the U.S. Olympic Hall of Fame in 1983. He won the Helms Trophy in 1948.

- He served as the U.S. Representative from California's 18th District (1967–75).

- Mathias was in active service in the U.S. Marine Corps 1954–56, and a Marine Corps Reserve captain from 1956 to 1965.

- He was a Goodwill Ambassador for the Department of State, for the international promotion of American youth programs.

- Mathias served as Deputy Director of Selective Service.

- He was director of the United States Olympic Training Center from 1976 to 1983.

- Mathias was director of the High Sierra Camp for Boys and the National Fitness Foundation.

- He was president of the American Kids Sports Association.

- Mathias is president of Bob Mathias, Inc., 1954–present.

- He played himself in *The Bob Mathias Story* (1954), a film based on his life.

- Mathias is the author with Bob Mendes of *Olympic Gold: Heartache, Guts and Glory at the Games*, and *A Twentieth Century Odyssey: The Bob Mathias Story*.

- At the Helsinki Games in 1952, Mathias won by more than 900 points, which was the largest margin in Olympic history.

- Mathias was never defeated in his 11 career decathlon competitions.

- In the 1956 interservice championships in Los Angeles, Mathias scored 7193 points without running the 1500-meter race.

- Mathias was the first Olympian to repeat a gold medal win in the decathlon.

Interview

"All my friends went out for sports, so it was just the natural thing to do."

Interviewer's Notes

During the summer of 1951, I was at the Marine Corps Recruit Depot in San Diego, along with Bob Mathias, who was also in "B" Company. During breaks, I visited with him, and we talked about his decathlon training.

One form of USMC recreation at that time involved a version of "beach ball." The idea of the game was to push a five-foot ball over the opponents' goal line, any way you could. Here was Bob Mathias, the world's greatest athlete, mixing it up in a no-rules free-for-all!

Years later, he graciously consented to sit down and talk again, this time about his experiences as an athlete and the values he drew from his experiences.

* * * * *

"I remember the first time I was aware that I could do something in sports," Mathias says. "I was about seven or eight, and my brother Gene was practicing high jumping down at the local grammar school, just a few blocks from our house. One of the teachers was helping him, and he got stuck on a certain height.

"'I can make it,' I told him, to which he replied, 'Get out of here, we're working.'

"When they weren't looking, I ran up and jumped the height. It amazed my brother, and he got mad at me," Mathias says, "but he told Dad and Mom about it anyway."

By the time Bob was 12, he could high jump 5 feet 6 inches.

Mathias says that he didn't get started in organized sports until he was fourteen and a freshman in high school. "My older brother went out for three sports in high school," he says, "so I did too. All my friends went out for sports, so it was just the natural thing to do.

"My parents didn't push me in sports. I knew that Dad had played a little football at the University of Oklahoma, but I didn't realize until later that he was a pretty good athlete. I never realized all this until my college days, when I asked him what he had done. "

Mathias's father, who was a doctor, had been a star tackle at the University of Oklahoma. He encouraged all three of his sons and his daughter to participate in sports.

Mathias attended high school in Tulare, California, a small farming community of about 12,000, where he lettered in football, basketball and track. He excelled in basketball and played all four years, averaging 18 points a game in his senior year.

His high school track coach, Virgil Jackson, believed that the talented Mathias could compete in the decathlon. Jackson encouraged him to compete in the Southern Pacific AAU Games in Los Angeles.

After winning the regional decathlon championship, Mathias traveled to Bloomfield, New Jersey, with the help of financial contributions from his hometown. There he won the National AAU decathlon championship, which constituted the trials for the 1948 Games.

Before the 1948 Olympic trials Mathias had never competed in the pole vault, long jump, javelin, or 1500-meter run. Mathias was so new to the decathlon events in 1948 that he left the discus throwing circle from the front, drawing a foul. He responded with the best throw of the day at 144'4". Mathias was so exhausted from the competition that he had to be awakened the following day to participate in the awards ceremony. When the 17-year-old Mathias was asked what he planned to do after winning the gold, he replied, "I'll start shaving, I guess."

After the first day of competition in London, Mathias was in third place. Cold weather and heavy rain delayed the second day's events, extending the competition from ten in the morning until ten o'clock in the evening. Mathias rallied through the bad weather to throw a 144-4 in the discus, his best event, which moved him into first place.

Drama heightened when it became apparent that light was needed to illuminate the foul line for the javelin throw. Cars were driven into the stadium, and drivers trained their headlights onto the infield. Through the cold and misting rain, Bob Mathias completed the final two competitions to become the surprise winner and the youngest decathlete in history. Back in Tulare, factory whistles and fire sirens sounded for 45 minutes when the town learned of the victory.

Mathias graduated from Tulare High School in 1948 and attended Kiski Preparatory School in Saltsburg, Pennsylvania. He enrolled at Stanford University and, at 6-foot-3 and 204 pounds, became a star fullback on the football team. He played in the 1952 Rose Bowl, which made him the only person ever to compete in a Rose Bowl and the Olympics in the same year.

Of his fellow athletes, Mathias says: "Through the years the camaraderie of old friends has meant a lot. You get to know the guys you play with, and stay close to them. In classes and school and work you make friends, but it's not the same as working out with somebody—tackling, blocking and competing. You develop a respect for these guys, who did the same thing you did."

"When I think about a club or fraternity of athletes," he says, "I think of the guys I played with in high school football, who are all very special to me. We all went through it together. Marine Corps boot camp is exactly the same thing—you all go through the same experience and that's your club. You get the *esprit de corps* from that one class in boot training—plus your hair cut!" he adds.

"The friendships I made in athletics extended to foreign competitors. I try to keep in contact with Heinrich, from the 1948 Olympics (Ignace Heinrich—France). He was second to me in the '48 Olympic Decathlon (Mathias 7139 points; Heinrich 6974 points), but he got injured in '52. Over the years I have run into him a number of times and have visited his home outside of Paris on several occasions. When he moves or changes addresses, he lets me know and when I move, I tell him about it.

"I also correspond with a friend from Iceland who was a decathlete. Occasionally in my travels I meet athletes from other countries that I competed against, and we stay close."

At the age of 21, Mathias retired from decathlon competition—an undefeated two-time Olympic winner, four-time national champion and three-time world record holder. He modestly says that although Olympians belong to an elite club, many talented athletes never get to compete in the games because of the timing (war years, boycotts, etc.).

When asked why he decided to run for Congress, Mathias says that he believed he had valuable experience to offer in the area of foreign policy.

"Because of my track participation, I had been all over the world by the time I got into politics," he says. "I made four trips for the State Department, and every summer between the Olympic Games, the AAU sponsored summer trips to Europe where I competed in every country. I had many friends overseas and knew the politics in their countries."

On a State Department trip to Taiwan, Mathias presented a javelin to C. K. Yang, then an unknown teenager. Yang attended UCLA and went on to set a world record score of 9121 in the decathlon. After this win, the scoring tables were revised to distribute points more evenly among events.

Mathias says that few people thought about a national training site for the Olympics when he first began competing in the Games. "In the '60s and '70s, however, they began to consider it," he says. "The Russian and German governments were greatly involved in training camps, sports medicine, and psychology. They built training facilities, and all their education sports programs were under the government regime. Our amateur athletic people heard about what they were doing, and there was a push to get something going."

He says that the 1976 Olympics were a wake-up call for the Olympic Committee. "They looked at the results of competition in Montreal and knew they had to do something. The question was how to do it within our system. One of the things that developed was the raising of money through corporations. From these funds and others, the Olympic Training Center (Colorado Springs, Colorado) got its start."

Mathias is a great supporter of the Olympic Festivals, originally called the National Sports Festivals. "It was a job opportunity program for Olympians who wanted to train, but who also had to work," he says. "They started lots of programs to compete with what the rest of the world does."

Mathias points out that the United States Olympic Committee, which now has its headquarters in Colorado Springs, Colorado, is a thriving organization. "They used to be more of a travel committee," he says, "making sure the team got to where they were competing. Now it is much different. Because of the Olympic festivals, 10,000 young people participate every summer. This kind of involvement generates a great deal of interest, especially for the young people who become aware of the Olympic movement every year. The participants will not all become Olympic champions, but they will be the best during that time."

Asked about the future of the Olympic Games, Mathias remains positive. "It is still the only event where young people throughout the world can get together. It's a great forum and I certainly hope they continue. Unfortunately it sometimes becomes a forum for political debate. The Games are just too good to allow the politics of any country to destroy them."

Mathias once said: "Years ago, in the days of the Greeks, wars were postponed to make room for the Olympic Games. In modern times, the Games have been postponed twice—to make room for wars."

He speaks proudly of a group called the International Olympic Foundation, located in Olympia, Greece, which holds yearly meetings to discuss Olympism. "The goal is to promote the Olympic ideals in every country," he says, "within the framework of the national governing body."

"For example, in the game of basketball, there are all kinds of divisions: men's, women's, age groups, and disabled. At the training center, the basketball association invites the wheelchair basketball people to come in. It is up to the national governing body to organize within their own ranks and create these different divisions. If there is interest in a disabled sport, those governing bodies support it. The training center is open to everyone."

Mathias believes that society and the schools should work hard to educate young people about the dangers of drugs and alcohol. "When they get older," he says, "especially in the pro ranks, if an athlete is tested and drugs are found in the system, they should be dismissed immediately from the team with no second chance. Most of our professional sports now allow more than one chance, usually with supervision. I doubt that this procedure is tough enough. The violators know about drugs. They should know that if they use them and get caught they will be kicked off."

Reflecting on his participation in sports and his later career, Mathias says, "Athletics have helped me in many ways. Participation gave me determination—the will to win. Things like that certainly carry over into the work world. You learn to do the best you can in everything."

It has been a special disappointment to Mathias to see schools drop physical education programs because of budget problems. "When I was going to Tulare High School," he says, "we went out every day for physical education. Sometimes it wasn't fun, but at least you got into the habit of exercise. Today young people don't form that habit of working out every day, because they don't have to do it in school. As a result they come home, watch television, and lose the great habit of learning about their body at an early age. Education is as important for the body as it is for the mind."

Mathias acknowledges the financial problems that face school districts. "I don't know what the answer is," he says, "but perhaps some of the money can be raised locally by charging admission to games."

Mathias believes that young people should have the opportunity to have fun in a variety of wholesome ways. "When I was in high school," he remembers, "my brother met a guy named Buzz Busick from Visalia, California. At that time, Buzz was probably the leading fly tier and fisherman in the whole San Joaquin Valley. During the summer we went on pack trips together. We traveled the John Muir Trail and the area east of Fresno. Buzz really knew the country, so we would get to lakes that people hadn't been to for years.

"Because of this early influence," Mathias says, "I later sponsored a youth camp east of Fresno for sixteen years [the High Sierra Camp for Boys]. The program everyone seemed to like best was the pack trip. Some of our target destinations were ones I had learned about years before."

Mathias tells about a man he met on an airplane several years ago. "I didn't recognize him," Mathias says, "but he said he wanted to thank me. When I asked him why, he replied, 'I went to your camp ten years ago.'"

"I told him how much I enjoyed those pack trips myself," Mathias says. "He went on to say that because of that experience, he developed an interest in mountain climbing. He said, 'I'm a doctor now and the first doctor to climb Mt. Everest.'"

Mathias adds, "I wish all youngsters could take a pack trip as part of their education."

9

Alfred "Al" Oerter

DISCUS THROW • FOUR GOLD MEDALS
Born 1936, Astoria, Queens, New York

Al Oerter is the only Olympian to win the gold medal in the discus throw in four consecutive Games (1956, 1960, 1964, 1968). Until Carl Lewis medaled in the long jump (1984, 1988, 1992, 1996) in four consecutive Games, Oerter was the only Olympian to win the gold medal consecutively in a single event. (Note: American Ray Ewry won four gold medals in both the Standing High Jump and the Long Jump in the Olympics of 1900, 1904, 1906, and the interim games in 1908.)

After an eight-year break from competition, Oerter missed a spot on the three-man discus team by inches. As events transpired, had he made the team, he still would not have had the chance to compete; the 1980 Olympics in Moscow were halted by the U.S. boycott of the games.

In May of that year at the age of 43, Oerter threw a record 211-5, exceeding his gold medal throw in 1968 by nearly five meters. Injury to his Achilles tendon prevented him from competing in the trials for the 1984 Olympics.

Career Acomplishments

- At 19, Oerter qualified for the U.S. team with one long throw.
- In 1956, at the age of 20 Oerter was the youngest Olympic world champion in the discus throw.
- He won the National Collegiate Discus Championships in 1957 and 1958.

- Oerter was the 1959 Pan-American Games Champion.
- When he threw the discus 200-5 in 1962, he was the first person to throw the discus more than 200 feet.
- He won discus titles at the United States National Championships in 1957, 1959, 1960, 1962, 1964, and 1966.
- He set Olympic records at every Olympics, exceeding his personal record three times in the 1968 Games, and winning the gold with a 212-6 throw.
- Oerter continued to compete as a nationally ranked discus thrower until 1985, retiring at the age of 49.
- He was inducted into the National Track and Field Hall of Fame in 1975, and the Olympic Hall of Fame in 1983. He won the Helms Trophy in 1964.
- Oerter was named by *Track & Field News* as one of the sport's two best Olympians. (The other was the legendary distance runner of the 1920s, Paavo Nurmi of Finland, who had become an Olympic champion in the 1500-meter and 5000-meter events in less than an hour at the 1924 Olympics.)

Interview

"The more I worked at throwing, the more I realized that if you truly enjoyed something, nothing external is necessary to make you continue training. You do it because you take pleasure in it and, regardless of the outcome, you continued to enjoy it."

Interviewer's Notes

My friend Fred Underwood, a colleague at McKendree College, agreed to me meet at LaGuardia Airport in New York and take me to Islip, Long Island, for an interview with Al Oerter. We had an interesting conversation at Al's home, and then Al had to leave for a scheduled workout in a local park. He graciously allowed us to go along. Fred and I leaned against a couple of trees and watched the warmup and the throws.

I was surprised to learn that there was an area in a public park in which to safely throw the discus. Land was at a premium and the neighborhood somewhat congested. But apparently Al was a favorite son, and this part of the park was personally reserved for the four-time Olympic discus champion to practice his throws.

Al Oerter (discus throw). (Courtesy Al Oerter and the University of Kansas Athletic Department.)

* * * * *

In our earlier conversation, I had asked Al about early influences that interested him in sport.

"My father was the greatest influence in my life when it came to sports," he says. "I started getting interested in athletics when I was about five years old, which pleased my father because he'd been captain of several sports teams in high school. He competed in sports we don't have today, such as team handball."

Oerter began lifting weights at the age of seven, and continued this exercise throughout his career. Six months after his comeback in the late 1970s he lifted at the same level as he did during the peak of his competition—pushing 200 kg on the bench press. By 1984 he was pushing 229 kg with two repetitions. He continued lifting weights until 2003, when heart problems prohibited him from this favorite exercise.

Oerter's father also played semipro baseball. When Al was 14, his father's teammate, future major league player Tony Cuccinnello, evaluated Al. Oerter remembers playing center field, and that when he threw to the pitcher or shortstop, it went out of the stadium!

Oerter also remembers that his mother was very protective; "but my father made the decisions when it came to sports, so I got involved early and enjoyed every minute," he says. "He didn't care if it was a team sport or individual, he just wanted me to participate.

"Team sports involved a group coaching effort," Oerter says, when asked to compare team and individual sport. "In my day, many coaches didn't get to know the athletes on their teams very well. Coaching in track and field was very different. You got to know the coach and the coach knew you: what you were like, if you were easily intimidated, if you dogged it or weren't living up to your potential. A track coach was someone who understood you and with whom you could have a very good relationship.

"I had only one coach in high school, Jim Fraley, who had been a track man at Emporia State University (1936). What he knew," Oerter says, "perhaps better than any man I've known, was how to instill the knowledge that you don't get something for nothing. He taught me how to work. If he thought I wasn't working to capacity, he let me know, and he wasn't above yelling."

Oerter remembers a competition in Glen Cove where the team didn't do very well. "After the meet he made the whole team run in front of the bus," he says, "all the way back to our high school! The team had dogged it and they realized it. It wasn't that he had to beat someone, but he took competition very seriously. He was really disappointed if we did not live up to our potential."

In the spring of 1952, high school sophomore Al Oerter was a sprinter and middle distance runner, working on the mile. At practice on a track at Sewanhaka High School, he picked up a discus that landed on the track and threw it back further than it had been thrown originally. Thus began a career that would span nearly four decades.

Oerter threw the lighter discus (wood and metal) used in high school 184-2, for a national prep record at the time.

During high school, Oerter thought his chances to attend college were slim. "My father could not afford to send me," Oerter says. "The most I could have done was to attend some small school here on the East Coast. But I won the state championship two years in a row, and during my senior year I set a national scholastic record in the discus. That event opened the door to some recruiting. There were many schools interested in track and field and the marks athletes were getting."

Oerter chose the University of Kansas because it offered an academic rather than athletic scholarship. "All I had to do was maintain grade point and I could continue to go to school," he says. "At that time, if you had an athletic scholarship and were injured, that scholarship stopped. There were no contracts for a year or any period of time.

"We had some very good teams at Kansas. Coach Bill Easton (Jayhawks track coach 1947–62) was a great recruiter. He could really bring in the people. There were no payoffs or that sort of thing. Instead, he showed us what he was building at Kansas—championship teams—and gave us a sense that we would be a part of it."

Millard "Bill" Easton is considered to have been one of the nation's best coaches at two universities—Drake and the University of Kansas. Inducted into the Coaches Hall of Fame in 1977, and the Track and Field Hall of Fame in 1975, he trained 32 All-Americans and eight Olympians. Three were world record holders: Al Oerter in discus; Bill Neider in shot put; Billy Mills in distance running.

"We had the opportunity to work with some very good people," Oerter says. "The school itself was very academic, and it was Easton's mindset that he wanted you first of all to get your education. When you got into competition, there were very few moments when he wanted you to go out and win, to just beat someone. But he did have a thing going with Tom Botts at the University of Missouri." Bott's longtime association with Mizzou [1946–72] resulted in 48 individual conference champions, 23 All-Americans, five national champions and two Olympians.

Oerter remembers that during Easton's first year at Kansas, the Missouri team rolled up a great number of points, and from then on Easton took that competition very seriously. "Against Missouri," Oerter says, "we rolled up the points or else—or in his words: 'I don't care if you're hurt, you're throwing!'" (This admonition would come back to drive Oerter a few years later, when the pain and the challenge were on the world stage.)

"Most of my long term friendships have been from athletics. Track and field folks tend to be different from other athletes, and put a great deal of thought into what they do. They would not continue in this sport if they did not truly enjoy it; this enjoyment comes from many sources. They work hard in a limited environment. They always try to get the best out of themselves. They don't point at a guy and say, 'I'm going to beat him.'"

Oerter believes that track and field is an introspective type of environment. "It either draws or produces athletes who know what they are about," he says. "Very little bothers them and they tend to take most things in life in stride. When the sport ends, most continue an active life style, which usually revolves around sport.

"On the other hand, when competition ends for a team athlete, there is a terrible void in his life. The mutual support required to excel in team sports is gone, and it's more difficult to go out in the world if that support isn't there."

Oerter observed that in the 40 years he's been competing, sports have changed from being an enjoyable hobby to a competitive business, tied to endorsements and great sums of money. He also remembers that throwers at the mid-point of the 20th century tried to achieve a style that looked graceful and relaxed.

When Oerter re-entered the sport in the late 1970s, throwers seemed more bulky and severe. "The camaraderie of competitors in past Games was also missing," he adds. "Today's competitors ordinarily do not speak to each other."

This is a loss for today's athletes, Oerter says, because he treasures the friendships he had with his competitors—teammates and rivals from around the world.

One example involved Olympic teammate Richard "Rink" Babka. Babka had defeated Oerter in the Olympic trials, Oerter's first defeat in two years. In the last round of finals at the Rome Games, Oerter trailed Babka by 15 inches. After a bad throw by Oerter, Babka told Oerter that his left arm was out of position.

With this bit of coaching, Oerter adjusted his throw and hurled a final of 194-2, a personal best and an Olympic record. He wished Babka luck in his final throw, but his teammate's effort fell short and Oerter won his second gold medal.

Asked about the application of what he learned in athletics to his later career, Oerter says: "I was in the computer field for 25 years. I worked for Grumman Corporation, where we had to have relatively short-term goals, with an eye toward something in the future. And short-term things were the most important. It was a good fit, because that's what track and field is all about. You don't go out to set world records; you try to improve on today's effort. If you do that enough times in a row, you will eventually get to the world's record."

When 20-year-old Al Oerter won his first gold medal at the 1956 games, he vowed to the press that he was not going to quit until he'd won five gold medals. Oerter said of his four Olympic victories that "the first was the most surprising, the second the most difficult, the third the most painful, and the fourth the most satisfying."

"When I came back into sport, some close friends told me I couldn't do it any more. I'd been away for eight years and if I went back, I'd just make a fool of myself. They were trying to protect me, because they thought I couldn't live up to what I'd done before. It would look like a lurch into the past; an attempt to recapture glory or status.

"I never understood their objections. The more I worked at throwing, the more I realized that if you truly enjoy something, nothing external is necessary to make you continue training. You do it because you take pleasure in it and, regardless of the outcome, you continue to enjoy it.

"It was very easy to get back into the swing of things. Throwing was something to be experienced, not endured. It was the journey and not the end result that became important."

In the 1960s, Oerter regularly threw distances of 230–262 feet in his training sessions. In competition, he threw 204-8¾ at the age of 50.

In 1984 at the age of 47, Oerter participated in an event where throwers were filmed with a high-speed camera. Take after take was ruined by broken film, but Oerter pushed harder every time, finally throwing 245 feet.

He won the World Veteran Championships in Eugene, Oregon, at the age of 53.

When asked if he was ever afraid of anything in sports, Oerter said "No, other than getting nailed by a javelin. I never experienced any feelings of fear about what would happen if I didn't compete well, or not win an event. I never feared that my family would cease to love me, or that my dog would bite me.

"I don't believe I have ever been compulsive about sports, because I never had a sense of having to win. When I won my first Olympic medal in 1956, it was a big surprise. I never had the feeling that this was my last shot. I came out of it with the gold and never had the feeling I would have to do it again. I relaxed, enjoyed the training, and that lasted a long time."

When Oerter, a sophomore at Kansas, went to his first Olympic competition in Melbourne in 1956, he had never won a major international competition. Oerter was ranked sixth in the world when he won the gold in Melbourne. His first throw of 184-10½ feet was a personal best and set an Olympic record. He finished with the three best throws. Not even the reigning world champion, Fortune Gordien, came within five feet of the winning throw. A year later, Oerter's goal of repeating his Olympic performance almost ended in a near-fatal auto accident. With determination and disciplined training he recovered completely, ready to compete again.

But Oerter was tenacious when it came to demanding the best of himself. During practice for the 1964 Games in Tokyo, he damaged cervical vertebrae and tore the cartilage in his left ribcage. He was advised by his doctors not to compete for at least six weeks. He rested for six days, then showed up for the preliminary round with a neck brace and ice packs.

Oerter threw a 198-8. In the finals, he was in third place going into his fifth throw. He threw off the neck brace and hurled the discus for a personal best of 200-1, an Olympic record, and good enough for the gold. His comment upon winning his third consecutive gold medal: "These are the Olympics. You die for them."

At the 1968 Olympics in Mexico City, Oerter again competed against his own injuries: a pulled thigh muscle and a chronic disk problem that required wearing a neck brace. Oerter threw away the brace after his second throw and wiped out the competition, increasing his personal best by more than five feet and finishing with the three best throws. For the fourth time, Oerter walked away with the gold and an Olympic record of 212-6.

Oerter says that when he reflects on his career in discus throwing, it isn't the number of medals of which he is most proud, but rather the length of time he participated in the sport. "I left the sport with the same attitude that I entered it," he says, "with the joy of throwing!"

At the age of 43, Oerter threw a 227-10½, a personal best. He placed fourth at the National Trials in 1980, qualifying as an alternate for the Moscow Olympics. The Games were boycotted by the U.S. team that year and, in 1984 at the age of 47, Oerter was unable to compete because of a strained Achilles tendon. If he had been able to compete in Los Angeles in 1984, he would have won a fifth gold if he had duplicated a throw earlier that year of 222-9.

10

Robert Eugene "Bob" Richards

POLE VAULT • TWO GOLD MEDALS

Born February 20, 1926, Champaign, Illinois

Bob Richards is the only man to have won two Olympic gold medals in pole vaulting (1952 Helsinki, and 1956 Melbourne). He won the bronze medal at the London Games in 1948, and is the only Olympian to have won three medals in the pole vault competition. In 1951, Richards became just the second man in history to vault 15 feet. He was an accomplished all-around athlete, winning national decathlon championships in 1951, 1954 and 1955.

At the University of Illinois, Richards tied for the National Collegiate pole vault title; during his time at Illinois, he won 20 National AAU titles—17 in the pole vault.

When Soviet athletes competed for the first time in the Olympics at the Helsinki games in 1952, Richards assumed the role of goodwill ambassador, arranging a visit between athletes from the U.S. and the USSR to help ease tensions during a critical time in the Cold War.

Career Achievements

- As a student at Bridgewater College in Virginia, Richards excelled in basketball and was an All Mason-Dixon selection in 1945.

- That same year, he captured titles in six track and field events at the 1945 Mason-Dixon meet: low hurdles, high hurdles, broad jump, high jump, javelin, and pole vault.

Bob Richards (pole vault). (Courtesy the University of Illinois Athletic Department.)

- Richards cleared 15 feet in 1951, the second athlete to do so. Cornelius Warmerdam had set the world's record in 1942, which stood for 14 years.

- Richards was a top contender from the U.S. for the 1956 decathlon, but was sidelined by injury at the trials.

- Gusty winds plagued the vaulters at the 1956 Olympics, but Richards cleared 14-11½ on his second try to win the gold.

- Richards was All-American in track and field for 11 straight years between 1947 and 1957.

- He is a member of the Illinois Hall of Fame, the Madison Square Garden Hall of Fame, and the National Track and Field Hall of Fame.

- Richards made three Olympic teams in two sports: pole vaulting and the decathlon.

- He was among the first class of athletes to be inducted into the Olympic Hall of Fame in 1983.

- Richards was winner of the Sullivan Award (which honors the year's outstanding amateur athlete) and the Helms World Trophy (1951).

- He won 26 national indoor and outdoor championships, and holds seven Hall of Fame Awards.

- Richards won the Masters Gold Medal in Pole Vaulting and broke the record in the Weight Pentathlon.

- Richards was the original Wheaties pitchman, known as "Mr. Breakfast of Champions." He was the first athlete to be featured on the front of a Wheaties box. Lou Gehrig was the first athlete to be pictured on the back. He set up the Wheaties Sports Foundation to encourage young people to aspire to fitness and participation in Olympic sports.

Interview

"One of the great lessons I've learned in athletics is that you've got to discipline your life. No matter how good you may be, you've got to be willing to cut out of your life those things that keep you from going to the top."

Interviewer's Notes

At the Track and Field Association/USA Meet in Atlanta, I was tossing the discus around, and I noticed another thrower warming up. We started throwing back and forth. The other fellow was smaller than most weight men, but his throws were very good.

From the discus ring area I heard "Richards! You're up! Let's go, Bob, it's your turn."

Without knowing it, I had been throwing with an Olympic champion. Bob was in a different age group, so I had the opportunity to see him win. I also overheard a young man, who was helping run the event, say "I never thought I'd meet the Reverend Bob!"

After the meet, I spoke to Bob Richards about doing an interview, and he had no problem with that. A few weeks later I arrived in Santos, Texas. Because it wasn't on my map, the folks at an area general store gave me directions to "Bob's place."

A few miles from town and down a half-mile lane, I came to a beautiful, partially completed home. It was much like one you might find on a movie lot for *Gone with the Wind*. Large white pillars at the front of the home supported a covered entrance. Under this weatherproof structure was a pole vault and high jump area. In front of these were areas for the shot put, discus and hammer. Bob showed me around his personal track and field set-up, and at the hammer ring he said, "All I have to do is throw over that tree out there and I'll have a world's record!"

Inside the home was a large room where we visited until well past midnight, doing discus spins on the plywood floor and discussing the finer points of the discus throw. His enthusiasm was contagious.

* * * * *

Asked to remember his earliest contact with athletics, Richards says, "Almost all of my early childhood memories are of sports. Both of my brothers were great athletes and both of my parents encouraged sports, so I grew up in an atmosphere that encouraged participation."

He continues by saying that as long as he could remember, athletics were part of his life. "When I was young," he remembers, "I lived in a fantasy world of sports. One of my favorite pastimes was throwing a tennis ball at the front porch steps and catching it, pretending I was a great pitcher. I played World Series after World Series, throwing that ball in there. If the ball hit the edge of the steps, it would be a fly or a grounder. If I missed, that would be a hit."

In the little parking areas between the sidewalk and the street in Champaign, Richards imagined himself playing football at the University of Illinois—catching the punts, dodging and twisting.

"In that same parking area," he says, "I constructed a jumping stage. I hammered nails into a tree and a telephone pole, and made a cross bar out of an old bamboo rod that was used for packaging rugs. I ran across the cinder road, planted the pole, and vaulted, landing on the bare ground. That's how I started pole vaulting."

The Richards family lived on the north side of town in Champaign, Illinois. "When I was a kid," he says, "it was a tough part of town, and we were tough kids. I remember when I was five, playing 'Kill the guy that's got it.' I tackled kids older than me, and once in a while I would get my chin torn off. But I learned to tackle big guys, and how to take a lot of knocks, bumps and bruises."

He tells about the time his father bought a vacant lot and planted 15 apple trees on it. "I wanted to make a place where I could play all the sports, so I sawed them all off. When he came home and saw what I'd done, he was pole-axed. He couldn't believe anyone would cut down his trees!

"He looked at me and said, 'Boy, you better be something.'"

Sports filled Richards' life and his imagination. "When my brother wanted to go out on dates," he remembers, "he brought me his assignments and made me do the typing. When I finished his work, I wrote sports stories. I added drama—three seconds left in the game, with guys stiff arming and dodging, almost being tackled, but managing to stay on their feet. The gun sounded and the crowd roared."

As a child, Richards was small and lacked confidence. "I only weighed 90 pounds as a ninth grader," he remembers, "and about 105 as a sophomore. Besides being small, I stuttered. But even at an early age, sports were forming my values. I believe, as did Plato, that you can't go on to higher reaches of the mind or spirit without physical development."

He believes that physical development gives a person a sense of their strength, "of being able to do things, take the knocks and bruises, get beaten, and come back. The muscles increase by doing work, and that work is all-important. You can't get endurance without hurting," he adds.

"Every great value I hold has come from sports," Richard says. "My religion, education and cultural upbringing are important, but for my development as a person, I credit sports.

"Plato said, 'You can see life written large in sport.' I can't imagine I would have been anything—in religion, the intellectual world, as a speaker, or leader—without the tremendous impact of the athletic world of my time."

Richards, an ordained minister, was often referred to as "the vaulting vicar." He was a theology professor in California when he qualified for the U.S. Olympic team in 1952 and is a charter member of the Fellowship of Christian Athletes (1954).

When asked about the current commercialism associated with sports, Richards says that money has become so involved that he can hardly watch the professionals.

"I see them bickering and quarreling over money all the time," he says. "You know, I used to laugh at Avery Brundage because he was an amateur. I went to the LaSalle Hotel and read all his books on amateurism. He wanted me to be a disciple. I used to laugh because I knew the average kid could not compete and be a pure amateur."

Avery Brundage, like Richards, was a graduate of the University of Illinois. He participated in the pentathlon and decathlon at the1912 Stockholm Olympics and worked in athletic administration for 40 years, serving terms as president of the AAU, the U.S. Olympic Committee, and the International Olympic Committee. He was known for his uncompromising stance on issues of doping, nationalism, politics, eligibility and commercialism, as they affected the quality of competition.

"Now I have seen the other side—the millions of dollars for those who dunk baskets, hit home runs, and run through the line. I feel like the sports world has been set back enormously by commercialism. If we don't do something to control the uninhibited demands of money and sports, the game will be ruined. Plain and simple, we have gone overboard on money."

In contrast to current standards, Richards challenges the justice of stripping Jim Thorpe of his gold medals because he was paid a meager amount to play baseball.

"I don't understand the use of drugs with sports," Richards says, "because sports give me a natural high. I love life. I'm a workaholic, and I love to go out there—to train and compete. I try to get in every track meet I can. In my spare time, I read every good book available."

"I cannot imagine any kid being susceptible to another person coming up with, 'Hey, here are some drugs; try this out and see if it won't wind you up.' I can't imagine anybody taking that stuff into their body."

"What does cocaine do for a person?" Richard wonders. "Some folks say it makes you feel good, or it relaxes you, or that it puts you on edge. A cup of coffee does that for me. It's the same thing with alcohol. It's easy for us to take off on drugs, but there are millions of people using alcohol the same way others use cocaine."

Richards remembers tough times in his early career. "I can remember dropping the football when I was an eighth grader, when hanging on to it would have meant winning the game. The lights hit me in the eye. The coach just couldn't understand how I dropped that football. I went through a lot of trauma about that.

"Another tough time came when the coach cut me from the basketball team. I cried a lot over that too. But all of the disappointments were part of hardening the will, the setting of the mind. I have not had any experience in sports that didn't serve a purpose or eventually bring about some good.

"I'm a senior citizen," Richards says, "but I'm out there every day, training. It reinforces all that is important to me: work, action, confidence and setting goals. Even when you are old and your legs hurt, you can overcome difficulties and go on. I owe a debt to sport—it is just part of me."

Richards says that he has nothing but the fondest recollections of his coaches. One of his best experiences happened when his high school coach called him up to the stage in assembly and gave him a pair of football shoes.

"When I first went out for football, there wasn't a pair of shoes that would fit me. I played football in junior high barefooted. The coach had a special pair made for me."

Richards continues: "The thing that amazes me about coaches is their ability to give of themselves. They get very little compensation. On the far end, of course, the really big coaches make a lot of money. But the ones I'm talking about help you when you are a kid. A lot of them are classroom teachers who do it for a few hundred dollars.

"A coach who influences a young person in sports is psychologically performing a role that cannot be duplicated," he says. "A minister or a teacher can't do it. In a way, it *is* teaching, only more than that. Coaching is a good model for teaching. It is the giving of oneself and relating to a kid on such a level, that he is willing to accept instruction—to grow, trust, and give himself to the mind of another.

"I have marveled at my coaches. I share a lot of what I have learned from them with my children. When I look back at the coaches who were willing to share just everything they had, I really admire them now. It is an act of unselfish love. The basic principle of American education is to develop the total person, a well-rounded individual, a good citizen, a worker. If we ever depart from that basic concept, we are in trouble."

In 1957, Richards wrote *The Heart of a Champion*, a best-selling inspirational book popular through the years with coaches and athletes. Today, he is a popular motivational speaker, addressing groups around the nation.

Richards has two sons who were pole vaulters. Brandon Richards held the National High School record.

11

David Wesley
"Wes" Santee

MIDDLE DISTANCES • OLYMPIC FINALIST IN
5000 METERS; 4 MINUTE MILE CONTENDER
Born March 25, 1932, Ashland, Kansas

Wes Santee, known as "The Kansas Flash," broke the American record for the mile race four times, with a personal best of 4:00.5 in Austin, Texas, as a member of the United States Marine Corps. As a sophomore at the University of Kansas, Santee was named outstanding meet performer at the 43rd annual Drake Relays. He anchored the distance relay team that raced to a meet record of 10:01.8.

Santee also anchored the four-mile relay, timed at 17:15.9—a Drake Relay record, an American record, and an American collegiate record. In the four mile relay Santee ran a 4.06.7 anchor mile, an outstanding feat for that time and a surprise upset for the favored team from Georgetown.

Santee broke the American record for the 1500-meter race twice. In 1954 he broke the World record, held by Gunder Hagg of Sweden for ten years, with a 3:42.8. In 1955, Santee joined other celebrated athletes whose amateur careers were ended prematurely (Jim Thorpe, Paavo Nurmi, Jesse Owens), when he was banned from competition for expense violations, which are no longer in force.

Career Achievements

- Santee was the only athlete to win the most outstanding performer award at the Kansas (1952, 1954), Drake (1954), and Texas (1955) relays.

- He received the prestigious Helms World Trophy in 1954.

- Santee broke the 20-year mile record set by fellow University of Kansas runner **Glenn Cunningham**.

- Santee ran 48 sub–4:10 minute miles—including his runs as anchor in relays—from his college years at Kansas until his suspension in 1956.

- His 42 open races surpassed the record of 28 set by Gil Dodds in the 1940s.

- In 1954 he broke Don Lash's record for the collegiate two-mile with an 8:58, in a meet with Arkansas and Drake.

- He won two conference cross-country championships and was NCAA cross-country champion in 1953.

- Santee ran on 23 championship relay teams, and anchored all but three. Eight of these wins set meet races, and three set world records.

- He won two Indoor 800-meter championships and one Outdoor 800-meter race.

- Santee defeated Lon Spurrier, the world's half-mile record holder, with a 1:48.4 at the Modesto Relays. He won the half mile at the Pacific Association AAU over Arnie Sowell with a 1:49.1.

- With a victory over two-time Olympic champion Mal Whitfield, Santee defeated the world's best half milers in his secondary distance.

- Within a year of graduating from the University of Kansas, Santee had completed the five fastest miles ever run by an American, and recorded 13 of the 17 lowest times on U.S. tracks.

Interview

"I really thought I would break four minutes—that I would be the first to do it."

Interviewer's Note

Wes Santee and I attended United States Marine Corps Reserves meetings together in Olathe, Kansas. At the base, we had a few "pickup"

Wes Santee (middle distances). (Courtesy the University of Kansas Athletic Department.)

softball games. Wes was a fair hitter and a good base runner. At that time I was a high school coach; I asked Wes if he would come up and work with my runners. He showed up on a rainy day and sloshed around a muddy track with some five-minute milers, offering advice and encouragement. There are still some of those trackmen who come up and tell me how good it felt to run with a World's Champion.

Wes was a straight talker and a doer. When he left active duty, he eventually became a full colonel in the Marines, and was elected president of the U.S. Marine Corps Reserve Officers Association. He fought a good battle to break the four minute mile—six tenths of a second would have done it.

* * * * *

As we sat down to talk about his early contact with athletics, Wes says that he heard very little about sports when he was growing up in Ashland, Kansas. "We had no radio except an old one that ran off a car battery. The radio was used mostly for the news, weather, and farm markets at noon time. The only sports I knew about at the national level were the New York Yankees and the great boxer, Joe Louis. We did listen to the World Series and the Louis fights," he remembers.

"The only magazine around our house was the *National Geographic*, and we subscribed to a paper called *The Cappers Weekly*. The newspaper had maybe one column, two inches long, about sports. I had very little exposure to information about sports figures of the past, such as **Glenn Cunningham.**

"Like all kids on the farm, I ran and had a football, and a baseball and bat. In school at the recess, there are only two things I can remember us playing very much. One was baseball and another was a game called 'tackle,' which was like football."

Early on Santee realized that among his classmates of 50 kids, he was probably third or fourth fastest. "If we ran around the block," he said, "I was the best. It really didn't mean a lot, except that as a kid we all liked to be best at something—running, throwing or hitting the ball. On the farm, instead of riding the tractor or truck back to the house, I would run. I had no brothers or sisters early in my life, so running by myself was a form of playing.

"As I came through the third, fourth and fifth grades, most of the activities remained about the same. I knew that if we ran very far I would be the best. I had no thoughts about college or the Olympics. When I was young, I thought about being a pilot. Out in the fields on the tractor I used to sing patriotic songs and dream about becoming a squadron pilot."

Santee remembers that in the small rural communities in Kansas, as in other parts of the country at that time, there was often a crossover in teaching between the high school and the grade school. Frequently, the high school coach taught a subject area in the high school, and physical education to the upper grades in the elementary school.

"The high school coach had to be smart," Santee says, "so in the fall he threw a football out, or a basketball, and that was his recruiting base for the next year. As far as having true physical education—we didn't have it. Our time was spent teaching the little kids football and basketball."

Santee says that his father had a third grade education, but his mother was educated, for those days. "My father was not supportive of any athletics at the school level," he remembers. "He'd had no experience with recess or gym classes, so he knew nothing about the work we were doing. During the summer, when we had hired hands (men who helped farmers with crops during the planting, tilling and harvest seasons), I would try to get them to throw the football to me or hit a baseball.

"One of our important races in school was 'Run to the elevator' (a grain storage facility near Ashland). I had passed everybody when we got there.

"Coach Murray said to me, 'You might be a good miler some day, maybe like **Glenn Cunningham**.'

"I didn't know much about sports history, but I did start picking up on who Cunningham was.

"In high school, things changed," Santee says. "A new boy came to school—a tall, skinny, pale little guy, who had been living in Africa with his missionary parents. He was a good runner and all of a sudden, I realized he was somebody who could challenge me.

"One day the coach asked me, 'How would you like to run a match race with Jack?'

"We went out to the half-mile horse track one afternoon during school and ran a mile. I ran a 5:17, the first race I had ever run that was timed. I beat Jack fairly easily, so that ended that debate.

"That spring the coach wanted me to be his miler. I told him I had to work and couldn't stay after school. He came out to the farm to see my father. My father was quick-tempered and the kind of guy that would say, 'Get the hell out of here!'

"My mother was exactly the opposite—she had baked donuts that night. I remember the coach coming after dinner," Santee says, "and we all sat around the kitchen table—in those old farm houses, you lived in the kitchen.

"I remember that it was tense. They liked him, so they wouldn't be nasty to him, but they also wouldn't say yes—it was this type of thing.

"I also remember him trying to break the ice by saying to my mother that her donuts were 'musty.'

"Well, she jumped up and wondered if the flour was bad and really took him seriously.

"Then he explained that 'musty' meant that he '*must* have some *more!*'

"The coach asked my dad if I could go to a track meet. My dad would not say 'yes,' but he also wouldn't say 'no.'

"After a while, the coach got up, said 'Thank you,' and left.

"The next track meet was three days later," Santee remembers. "He told me, 'I'm coming out to get you. Get up and get your work done and I'll pick you up at 7 A.M.'

"I got up at five and did all kinds of work, got dressed and left before my parents got up. I left a note telling them that I had gone to Anthony, Kansas, to the relays. I took third in the race.

"When I got home, Dad was waiting up for me. He said, 'If you and the school have time to go to a stupid track meet, you have time to finish up the plowing.'

"I went to bed, got up at 4 A.M., and went out and plowed for two days, trying to get the work done so I could go back to school. The coach called and wanted my dad to take me to a track meet that night in Meade, Kansas.

"I had been working day and night, but my dad took me and I just barely got beat by a senior. I was so tired I could hardly walk. After that my father would say I could go to the meets, but demanded a lot of work in return.

"In those days, the superintendent of schools wasn't off in some building twenty miles away from the school system. He was right on the scene and knew what was going on. He called me in and said, 'If you will do your classroom work at home, I will make sure you get the lessons and none of the teachers will harass you for being out of school.'

"So basically, I went through four years of high school, lettering two years scholastically and four years with an athletic letter. I missed school somewhere between a third and half the time. As long as I was on that schedule, my father did not object, and since the superintendent did not object, I went on to break Glenn Cunningham's high school record some twenty years after he had set it.

"Years later Glenn, Jim Ryun and I ran a lap at the Kansas Relays. I had a terrific time. It was interesting to see how size makes a difference. Ryun was 6'3", I was 6'1", and Glenn was 5'8". If you go back 35 years, the difference between Cunningham and Ryun makes Cunningham's times even more phenomenal.

"During my freshman year, I ran seventh at the state track meet, and won it my sophomore year. My junior year I was sick, and as a senior I was beaten by Billy Tidwell from Kiowa.

"I had met Bill Easton, the track coach at Kansas, and Dutch Lonberg, the athletic director, my junior year. In those days, the athletic director would speak at an athletic banquet; that's how they did their recruiting. I went to Kansas as a high school senior. My dad brought me there to run in the State XC Championships.

"Easton told me that I had a scholarship. My dad never gave me any money and never assisted in any way, so when I came to the University of Kansas, I was very dependant on Coach Easton. There was a couple in Wichita who had a brother in Ashland. They knew I didn't have any clothes or spending money, so every once in a while, I would get a five dollar bill from them.

"I sold programs at the football games. Some days I would make forty or fifty bucks. That was really great. I got a job waiting tables in a sorority house. Ultimately I was almost adopted by the Easton family. At this time they were like my parents. There was a warm feeling being around them.

"When I was a junior, Easton put together a relay team for the Drake Relays. We were running so far behind, if I'd had a jet, I still wouldn't have won. I walked over to the stand and told Easton, 'Let me run something else, Coach. There's no point in running a four minute mile on the end of a losing relay.'

"He didn't agree, and told me to go on and run. We ran another relay and the same thing happened. At this point, I was really mad—not at him, but at the whole team.

"As I was walking back to the stands, he asked, 'What's the matter?'

"I told him that I didn't want to talk about it, and walked away. He sent one of the fellows in to ask me if I would like to run on the mile relay team. I told him 'No.' Then three members of the team came up and told me that they thought we could win it. Oklahoma had the best mile relay team. They decided to run their fastest runner, Cox, third, to get a lead for their anchor man.

"Easton put me in the third position. Cox got the baton three or four yards ahead of me and I took off after him. I caught him on the back stretch. I started to pass him like a miler, not a quarter miler. When I went past him he changed gears and we went around that track elbow to elbow, and I just edged him on the handoff. My time was 47.4. We ended up winning the mile relay.

"Afterward nothing was said to me. The following Wednesday, Easton sent word that he wanted to see me. I hadn't thought much about being disrespectful; I had just been mad. He and I sat down that day and had our first long talk about where I was going, beyond track."

Tom Rosandisch, president of the U.S. Sports Academy, was the Marine Corps coach at Quantico when I was on that team. I had kept all of the Easton workouts a year before I went on active duty, so when I joined up and ran on the team, it was an easy transition.

"In 1952, I met Landy and Bannister. They have a different system of competition in those countries than we do," Santee says. "I ran every weekend, but the Europeans and others would train for two or three weeks, and then run.

"In the quest for the four minute mile, I had to approach it a lot differently than runners from other countries. I was usually younger than most of the foreign runners. For example, when I was a 19-year-old freshman in the 1952 Olympics, the AAU put me in the 5000 meters instead of the 1500, and I had to run against athletes in their thirties.

"I really thought I would break four minutes—that I would be the first to do it. In Britain, they brought all the best athletes together and trained for a staged goal—to be the first to break the four minute mile. They planned for it. I couldn't get anyone to be a rabbit (a pace setter). I like to think that if we would have brought some of our good runners together to push me for three quarters, I could have broken the barrier.

When the three contenders were chasing the four minute mile, they headlined the newspaper, and were featured in magazine articles and interviewed on sports programs.

The mile race was a featured event run in front of sellout crowds at the major track arenas of that time, including Boston Garden and Madison Square Garden. The four minute mile requires athletes to run four laps averaging 15 miles per hour. This achievement was not only thought to be unattainable, but medical experts believed the attempt to run it would jeopardize an athlete's health. Roger Bannister broke the four minute mile on May 6, 1954, with a time of 3:59.4 on the Iffley Road Track in Oxford, England. A few weeks later in Turku, Finland, John Landy of Australia broke Bannister's record with a 3:57.9. At the Vancouver Empire Games in August of 1954, Bannister again defeated Landy with a time of 3:58.8. Landy ran a 3:59.6, which made this the first time two runners had broken the four minute mile in the same race. (After winning the 1500-meter race in the European Championships, Roger Bannister returned to the medical school and became a neurosurgeon. He was later knighted by Queen Elizabeth.)

Today, despite the increased interest in jogging and running, there has been a decline in interest in the mile, due in part to an increased focus on cross-country and marathon races.

According to track journalist Marc Bloom, U.S. participation in the mile was affected when shoe companies stopped supporting distance runners. Sheer dominance of the mile event by Kenyan athletes may have discouraged some potential milers, and U.S. coaches, afraid of pushing their athletes too hard, developed more cautious training methods.

"The problem was that in the 1950s it could be difficult to find someone who could run under three minutes for three quarters," Santee says. "So there was a real handicap in setting up the race that Bannister ran. I don't fault them for it. If our NCAA team and the AAU had said, 'Let's be the first to break the barrier by funneling in the good runners at the Compton Relays, or someplace with a hot track,' it would have happened.

"When I was a junior they brought in runners from Finland and Belgium to run against me. Had those guys set up the race, I would have beaten them, whatever the time it took. They ran a 2:05 first half. I took off on my own and ran the fastest second half ever in 1:59.

"When I was a freshman I was not eligible to run in any NCAA meets, because freshmen were not eligible. After the NCAA meet, I was entered in the AAU meet. The secretary typed the entry on University of Kansas forms instead of on plain papers, as an unattached entry. I went out and ran, and as a freshman, I whipped every opponent in the 5000 meters. The only runner who beat me was Fred Wilt from Indiana.

"Bill Easton was criticized for allegedly trying to run me as a University of Kansas student. They then tried to disqualify me for a year. Fortunately, Easton survived, but I was not eligible for the National Championships my senior year."

Santee was then faced with the problem of how to qualify for the 1952 Olympics. "I wasn't in the military," he says, "so I couldn't run in the All-Service Championships. In the NCAA, I ran the 5000-meter and won it. I was now qualified. The following weekend I ran the 1500-meter, my favorite event, and I won that going away. At the Olympic trials I took second in the 5000, but when I was on the track warming up for the 1500, the officials took me off, telling me I couldn't run both.

"Easton came down and said, 'Wes, I'm sorry. I've been in a meeting for an hour with these people trying to convince them to let you run.'

"With no advance warning, I was stuck in the 5000 meters, running against some good mature foreign runners—and I was only 19 years old.

We had never won the 5000 until Billy Mills (also from the University of Kansas) took the gold in Tokyo. In the 1500 meters, Jose Bartel of Luxembourg won, Bobby McMillan of Occidental College was second. I had easily beaten both of them every time I ran the 1500.

"The next year I went to Europe with the U.S. track team and was supposed to be there two weeks. But I stayed in Europe all summer, along with Mal Whitfield, Parry O'Brien, Ernie Shelton, and J. W. Mashburn. We ran in almost every country in Europe—on an average of every other day. Try that one on for size!

"Some members of the (Kansas City) Royals baseball team said I didn't understand playing every day. But I told them that in every country in which we competed, they saved their best for us every other night. I didn't lose many races, but I had to set new American records just to win; that's how tough the competition was.

"The winter of my senior year I was going to be running indoors, and the Pan American Games for 1955 were coming up. Unless somebody beat me, I would be the number one miler at the Pan American Games. The national championships were scheduled for Madison Square Garden. If we qualified, we went up to Pan American Games.

"There was a conflict. The week after that meet there was the indoor meet in Milwaukee, and the Pan American Games were the following week. I wrote to Dan Ferris, who was then the head of the AAU. I said, 'Dan, if I win at the indoor and am eligible for the Pan Am Games, can I leave the team and go to Milwaukee and run?'"

Ferris wrote back and said that it would be all right. I ran in Madison Square Garden, won the mile and was automatically on the team. I turned in my papers, got on the plane and flew back to Kansas. On Monday morning, I was kicked off the Pan American team for leaving the team.

"It was ridiculous because I had permission to leave. I produced the letter from Ferris, at which point they realized they were wrong. They went to Dutch Londberg, who was the Director of Athletics at the University of Kansas, and made a deal with him. If I would go to Houston, Texas, two days later, and run in an exhibition to help them raise money for the Pan Am Games, I would be put back on the team.

"In order to save face and keep peace in the family, I agreed to fly to Houston to compete against the same people. I won that race in 4:05, got right back on the plane, flew back to Kansas, and picked up my gear to run again in Milwaukee—Saturday, Wednesday, and Saturday races.

"After Milwaukee I was back on the plane to Mexico City, and lost in a photo finish at the Pan Am Games." Juan Miranda of Argentina took the gold in the 1500 with a time of 4.53.30, and Santee took the silver with a 4.53.44.

"Harold Berlinger, a top AAU Official in San Francisco, told me about a meet being approved by the *San Francisco Chronicle*. He said, 'You come out here and we'll have a great meet.'

"The meet was scheduled on a Saturday night, and I told Harold I couldn't come, as I had a conflict. I had promised the previous year to go to Reading, Pennsylvania, and do a benefit program—a running exhibition to raise money for a Catholic high school. There were no jets in those days, so I couldn't get from Pennsylvania to California in time. Physically I could have run both, but the transportation wasn't possible.

"I went to Reading and was reimbursed $400 in expenses. Some 10,000 people showed up and we raised a lot of money. The following week, the San Francisco Chronicle wrote an article about how much money I was making in track and field, and that I should be barred. This triggered an investigation by the Missouri Valley AAU.

"I never received expense money except from an AAU official," Santee says. "All of these promotions were by AAU officials, and they were the ones who gave the expense money to me. The rule book said train, transportation, and 12 dollars per day, but I reminded them that I had to fly in order to get to the meets where I was scheduled to run. I couldn't do it any other way.

"The voting result was 21 to 7 not to discipline me," Santee says. "The rule book said that if either side did not agree with the majority decision within ten days and the posting of 50 dollars, they could appeal to the National AAU. Ten days became a month, and I thought it was all over. But after the ten days were up, one of the seven appealed because he did not like the decision. I was not allowed to testify on my behalf when the national group met, and in the end I was banned for life.

"By now I was in the Marine Corps. General Pollock was a big sports fan, and did not like the decision. He helped me get the services of an attorney, and we got an injunction against the AAU. It was temporary, but it kept being extended.

"I ended up with three temporary extensions. Because of this I was allowed to run while I was in the Marine Corps. The AAU told me that they couldn't stop me from running, but they went to all the coaches on the East Coast and told them if that if any of their athletes ran against me, they would declare them ineligible.

"So I ran the official race. All the guys in the military ran against me, and then they had a separate race for the others. In Madison Square Garden, night after night the crowd would stand for 11 laps and cheer for me."

When Santee's attorney pressed for a permanent injunction against the AAU, Santee declined to take the case further, fearing that he might implicate other athletes as part of his defense.

"Today, marathoners get $25,000–50,000 to run," he says, "and they allow athletes to represent businesses. The top miler now may get several thousand dollars a race. When you look back at how restricted we were, and how well the system was working, I'm a little surprised at how well we did.

"I have never turned down a school that asked me to come and talk to them, hold a clinic, or whatever," Santee says. "Sometimes I have been paid, and sometimes I haven't. It was never an issue with me.

"My biggest ambition in track was to knock off the four minute mile, no question about that. The toughest runner I competed against was Gunnar Neilsen from Denmark. I lost to Gunnar twice. However, I did set the world's indoor mark in a race against him, and going to the Olympic Games was my biggest thrill."

Memorabilia from Wes Santee's career is located in the Ashland, Kansas, Pioneer-Krier Museum, along with that of four other famed citizens from Ashland: Harold Krier, Jesse Clair Harer, Jay Berryman, and Rodney Hardesty.

The Four Minute Mile (coproduced by ABC/BBC) profiled Santee, Roger Bannister, and Chris Chataway of Great Britain; John Landy of Australia; and Denis Johannson of Finland in their race to break the record.

The Perfect Mile, from the same company that produced the movie *Seabiscuit,* was scheduled for release in 2004 and features the efforts of Santee, Bannister, and Landy to be the first to achieve the mile record. The movie is directed by Frank Marshall, a runner himself and a member of the U.S. Olympic Committee.

12

Jackson Volney Scholz

SPRINTS • GOLD MEDAL—200 METERS;
SILVER MEDAL—100 METER DASH
Born March 15, 1897, Buchanan, Michigan
Died October 26, 1986, Del Ray Beach, Florida

Jackson Scholz was born the year after the revival of the ancient Olympic Games in Athens, Greece. He became the first Olympian to reach the sprints finals in three different Games (1920, 1924, and 1928). He won a gold medal in 1920 as part of a 4 × 100 relay that included Charlie Paddock, Loren Murchison, and Morris Kirksey.

Scholz captured the gold in the 200-meter race at the Paris Games in 1924, with a 21.6—beating out Charlie Paddock, who held the world's record of 21.0. In one of sports history's more exciting races, Scholz lost the gold in the 100-meter dash to Harold Abrahams of Great Britain. His silver medal win was clocked at 10.8, two-tenths of a second behind Abrahams, who finished in 10.6. Charlie Paddock, the world's record holder in the 100 meters at that time with a 10.2, placed fifth in the race.

Career Achievements

- Scholz was inducted into the U.S. Track and Field Hall of Fame in 1977.

- A star athlete at the University of Missouri, Scholz won the AAU national championship in the 220-yard sprint in 1925.

- Scholz and his running mates (Paddock, Murchison and Kirksey) set a world's record of 42.4 with their 1920 gold medal win in the 4 × 400 relay.

119

- He placed fourth in the 100-meter race at the Antwerp Games in 1920, and fourth in the 200 meters at the 1928 Games in Amsterdam.

- Scholz was named in *Sports Illustrated*'s "50 Top Athletes of the 20th Century" (Missouri).

- Scholz competed in fifteen foreign countries including New Zealand, Japan, and most of the western European countries.

- In 1928 Charlie Paddock, Scholz's teammate on the gold medal 4 × 400 in 1920 and a star sprinter himself, listed Jackson Scholz at number four on his list of the top ten sprinters competing in America that year. Scholz was running for the New York Athletic Club at the time.

Interview

"Coach Schulte saw me walking across the street and he yelled at me, 'Toes in, Jack. Toes in!'"

Interviewer's Notes

I had written to Jackson Scholz about a possible interview. He wrote back that he wasn't in very good health, but if I wanted to come and visit, that would be fine. I went to Del Rey Beach, Florida, where Scholz was living in a retirement home. He had a beautiful apartment, where we sat and visited for some time. We talked about the University of Missouri and some of the people we both knew that he had competed with.

Scholz lit up a cigar about as big as he was, and we continued our visit. At noon he took me to lunch, sprinting around corners in his three-wheeler like a pro. After we got our food, he led me over to a table in the corner, saying, "Let's get away from these old people." (At the time Scholz was 89.)

After lunch we returned to his room. Scholz had been a noted author of children's books, and had 25 or more on a shelf. He had a duplicate— a novel about golf—and he gave it to me. He talked about how he came to choose journalism as a career, and about Charlie Paddock from his competitive running days. He mentioned the movie *Chariots of Fire*, which he had never seen.

"There was a lot about how I thought or felt in the movie, according to those who saw it. How could they possibly know what I was thinking or feeling?" he asked me.

Jackson Scholz (sprints), September 9, 1924. (Courtesy Jackson Scholz.)

I enjoyed my visit with Jackson Schulz, and was saddened to learn from the newspapers a few days later that he had died in the evening, shortly after we had talked.

* * * * *

Asked about his early life, Scholz said, "I was raised in St. Louis, Missouri. When I was in high school, one of the local papers had a contest sponsored by the *Los Angeles Times*; the winners would get a free trip to California."

Scholz, who weighed about 85 pounds at the time, entered the contest. "They thought they had a particularly fine sprinter," Scholz says. "They put me in a tryout with him, and I beat him. Of course, they couldn't believe it so I had to run him again, and I won that race too. That's when I discovered that I could sprint." Scholz won the contest and a two-week trip to Catalina.

"My parents were very cooperative concerning my track participation," he remembers. "They definitely backed me. By the time I graduated from high school, I was really interested in track. I enrolled at the University of Missouri, where they had many fine athletes at that time. Brutus Hamilton was a good friend of mine. He was a decathlon man and just missed the gold medal in the Olympics. In 1952 he was the coach of the Olympic team for the Helsinki Games.

"Bob Simpson was also on the team. He was the finest hurdler in the world, and I competed in his shadow. I was just a shade faster and quite a bit shorter than Bob." (A track star at the University of Missouri, Simpson was known in his time as "Missouri's Greatest Athlete.")

"Schulte was our coach at Missouri—a very fine man, who kept an eagle eye on us. I remember once when he saw me walking across the street and he yelled at me, 'Toes in, Jack. Toes in.' I had a tendency to toe out a little when I was running. He was a fatherly type person and we were all very fond of him."

Henry F. (Indian) Schulte was head coach at the University of Missouri before moving on to the University of Nebraska. During his career at both schools, he raised the level of participation in track and field, and won four consecutive Missouri Valley championships for Nebraska. He built an indoor track under the Nebraska stadium, which allowed athletes to train during the winter months for the spring season. In his time, Schulte was regarded as one of the leading authorities in track and field.

"The work we did in those days, both in the classroom and on the track, was more practical," Scholz says. "We had practice every day but, despite all this and my classes, I found plenty of spare time. In those days we believed the best training was not to overdo things. If you were good enough and you tried to get better, you might just get hurt.

"I think one of the objections to [present-day] high school track coaching is they often work their athletes too hard. If a sprinter can do a good 100 meters, they push him to run the 400 meters—that sort of thing. I honestly believe that college athletic programs burn out a lot of the young athletes. They never have a chance to reach their potential, because they overdid it in high school.

"We did all our running exclusively on cinders," Scholz says, "which was not the best surface we could have run on. The tracks were unpredictable: They were hard, soft or loose. There is no question that the modern tracks bring out the best in a man. Another thing we never bothered with was weights, but we did a lot of stretching exercises every practice. Our training also emphasized high kicking, which was believed to be essential in keeping the hips limber.

"When I started at Missouri, I didn't know what course of study to take. After considerable thought, I decided on Agriculture. I thought it would be a nice idea to sit around on the porch in a pair of jumpers and let the foreman report to me about what was going on. That was about all I knew about it," he laughs.

"We were required to spend a certain amount of time on a farm, actually doing the work. I tried this out and found it was not for me, so I switched to journalism. The University of Missouri was considered one of the best journalism schools in the country at that time.

"I started writing short stories toward the end of my schooling. A close friend of mine, who had just graduated, had taken a short story course. I got a very exciting letter from him one day, saying he had sold his first short story. Well, I thought, if he can do it, so can I. I rented a typewriter and went to work.

"I tried to sell these stories for quite a while and received dozens of rejections. Another of my friends knew a person working with a short story magazine published by Street and Smith. The editor asked my friend for a biography. Now this fellow didn't know much about writing, so he gave the editor my name. After an interview and an article of some 110,000 words, they took everything I wrote."

After Scholz completed a degree in journalism at the University of Missouri, he competed for the New York Athletic Club, worked for the United Press, and eventually became a noted freelance writer. He was well known as a writer of sports stories for young teens and adults. An avid golfer with an interest in all sports, Scholz used football, baseball, or golf themes for his stories. Copies of titles such as *End Zone, Rookie*

Quarterback, The Big Mitt, and *Batter Up* are considered rare and collectible. Several, considered classics in young adult literature, have been reissued. Critics of his writing for adults praised his precise knowledge of sports and the swift movement of his storylines. Between 1935 and 1969, Scholz published 29 books. In his career as a journalist, he wrote more than 300 short stories and novelettes in magazines.

After graduation in 1919, Scholz was commissioned in the U.S. Navy and became a pilot, flying the Sopwith Camel. This plane, perhaps the most famous of the WWI fighter planes, was a single-seater, named by its flyers for the hump over the breeches of the two front machine guns. "The Armistice had been signed by this time and my aviator experiences were uneventful," remarked Scholz.

"The 1920 Olympics were held in Antwerp," he continued. "Here in the States, we had no training camp, and there was really nothing to prepare us for the Games. They sent us over in an old troop ship that had just arrived, delivering a group of soldiers returning from Europe. They packed us in that thing and sent us over. The facilities we had on the ship were pretty rudimentary. But when we got to Antwerp [Belgium] the facilities were miserable.

"The coaches we had were very casual about it all. There seemed to be little importance attached to those Olympics. There was nothing overtly political, however, and in that respect it was quite nice.

"At Antwerp I competed in the 100 meters and placed 4th. I ran in the 4 × 100-meter Relay with Charley Paddock, Loren Murchinson and Morris Kirksey and we took the gold."

Paddock, known in the 1920s as the World's Fastest Human, was a three-time Olympian and gold medal winner in the 100 meters. He held world records in the 100 and 200 meters. He later became a movie actor, but was killed in a plane crash while serving in the Marines in World War II.

Morris Kirksey, another member of the winning 4 × 400 in 1920, was also part of the U.S. gold medal rugby team that year, and won a silver medal in the 100-meter dash. He is one of only four athletes to win gold medals in two different sports. He won the IC4A 100-meter championship in 1922 and 1923.

Loren Murchison, the fourth member of the 4 × 400, won the 60-yard dash championship in the U.S. Men's Indoor Track and Field competitions in 1919 with a 6.6, a 6.3 in 1920, 6.4 in 1922 and 1923, and a 6.6 in 1924.

"In 1924, our training was quite different," Scholz says. "The New York Athletic Club sent us to Travers Island, a sort of a country estate, and they took really good care of us. They did everything possible to get us ready for the Games. Robbie Robinson, from Pennsylvania, was our coach, and he did a good job preparing us.

"When we arrived in Paris, there was a type of Olympic Village arrangement, and everyone made a great effort to make us comfortable. There was much fun and excitement. Douglas Fairbanks, Mary Pickford and Maurice Chevalier did their best to support us. [Fairbanks, Pickford and Chevalier were well known actors, whose professional entertainment careers spanned several decades.]

"In 1924, England made a great effort to train Harold Abrahams for the sprints. He beat me in the 100 meters by about 2 ft. I beat him quite easily in the 200 meters. Charlie Paddock was a close second and Eric Liddell finished third in that race."

Liddel, featured in the movie, *Chariots of Fire*, was a prominent Scottish athlete, the son of missionaries to China. He refused to compete in the 100-meter race at the Paris Games, because it fell on Sunday, but won a gold medal in the 400 meters and a bronze medal for the 200.

"The *Chariots of Fire* film was about the 1924 Olympics," Scholz says, "but I have never seen the movie. I was not interested in someone else portraying me and trying to think like I did. I have a cassette of it—they sent it to me, but I have never played it. I saw some of the short reviews and there were so many discrepancies that I lost interest.

"For instance, I was supposed to have handed a note to Eric Liddel before a race. I didn't even know the guy. They just stuck that in. I was more casual about religion than to hand a note containing a biblical quotation to a competitor." Scholz's name was also mispronounced throughout the film, and he did not meet the Prince of Wales.

Scholz continued, "I trained again for the team in 1928, and my time in the finals tied me for third place. I was told much too late that there would be a run off for the bronze medal. I was tired of running—it was my third Olympics—and as a matter of fact, I wasn't interested in a third place anyway.

"I went to the Captain of the Team, who happened to be Douglas MacArthur. I talked to him about it and he told me I didn't have to run if I didn't want to, so I didn't."

In 1927 MacArthur formed the American Olympic Committee (AOC), the governing body for American athletes. MacArthur, a World War I war hero, was later the Supreme Allied Commander of Troops in the Southwest Pacific in World War II and Supreme United Nations Commander in Korea.

"Of course, one of the big advantages of having competed in the

Olympics was that you were invited to compete in foreign countries," Scholz says. "When the 1924 Games were over, four of us traveled to Sweden. They entertained us elaborately—so elaborately that they would pass around cigars after every dinner. Only one of our group smoked cigars and the rest of us would take one for him. I thought—well, this is rather silly—let me try one and see what it does, and I have been smoking them ever since.

"I also spent two months in Japan after the 1924 Olympics. Two other Americans—Emerson Norton and A.R. Sparrow—and Jonni Myyra from Finland also made the trip. That voyage took us around the world, because we sailed from Marseilles, in France."

A magazine printed in Japan at that time commemorates the athletes' visit with photographs and addresses by the Olympians. In his remarks, Scholz said:

> Friends and fellow athletes. Although at a meeting of this sort, we are handicapped somewhat by being unable to speak each other's language, we may find a great deal of satisfaction in the knowledge that there is being developed a language common to all nations, which may be understood and enjoyed by everybody, irrespective of his race. I refer to the language of athletics, a language which does not have to be spoken by the lips, but which, nevertheless may be easily learned by all on the field of competition.... The language of athletics is based upon the simple code, 'the game for itself.' It is the aim of each country, desirous of learning this language to send their men into competition with this fundamental idea uppermost in their minds—to lose with a smile, but above all, to win like a gentleman.

The other athletes expressed hope that competition on the athletic field would supplant violence of the battlefield—a hope that would be dashed by the onset of a second world war, only a few years after their visit.

"After a wonderful visit there," Scholz continues, "we spent several months in New Zealand, where we also competed and held clinics. So you see, competing has its advantages.

"My thoughts about future Olympics are strictly a matter of opinion. I'm sure the games will continue, but whether there will be an improvement, I don't know. Prominent athletes, even in my day, would not compete without having some assurance that they would receive travel expenses and that sort of thing. What we got wasn't much, just enough to eat and hotel expenses. You certainly could never live on it.

"It's likely that we will see more professionalism among our athletes. Obviously, politics play a big part, just as they have since our first Modern

Games in 1896. Countries who wish to sponsor the Games must have good facilities these days to attract the competitors from the various countries. Both the athlete and the country want to gain prestige.

"One of the things I am often asked is how I would compare today's athlete with the athlete of yesterday," Scholz says. "I have always maintained that they were just as good, especially in track and particularly the sprinters. I believe they were equally competent and perhaps better, because these days athletes run with starting blocks, improved tracks and proper timing.

"We had no opportunity to compete under those conditions. When you were getting ready for a race you just dug a couple of holes in the ground—there were no starting blocks. This suggests to me that a runner might lose several tenths of a second right there. Travel was quite different too. Most of it was done by train, hundreds of miles of it.

"As far as my athletic friends go, most of our association was on the track. Charlie Paddock, for instance, ran against me many times. He advertised himself as 'World's Fastest Human,' but I competed against him 15 times—beat him 12 times and tied one. Charlie was from California and attended USC. We were the same height, about 5'8". But Charlie had a more muscular body and a stocky build. He was a great runner. In the 1920 Olympics, he won the 100 meters. I have not had many opportunities to visit with many of my friends these past few years. Many of them are dead."

When Scholz was asked about what he had gained from participating in athletics, he said: "There are many things to be learned from competing in sports. Of course, body building and that sort of thing was beneficial. Morally, there were benefits gained from the competition itself. When I was writing I had deadlines to meet and my experiences in sports definitely helped me in that way. Track has also probably been beneficial to my health—I will be 90 next March.

"Some people call me a hero, and it embarrasses me," he says. "The whole thing depends on a natural ability to start with. If you have it, you have it. A person doesn't deserve all the credit. You simply have to admit that you are talented in that respect and don't deserve any particular credit for that sort of thing—it just comes natural. It always looks so awesome when it's the other fellow."

13

William Anthony "Bill" Toomey

DECATHLON • GOLD MEDAL

Born January 10, 1939, Philadelphia, Pennsylvania

Bill Toomey won the gold medal in the decathlon at the Mexico City Olympic Games in 1968, with a record-breaking 8193 points. A consistent competitor and dedicated athlete, Toomey holds unbroken records for five consecutive wins in the U.S. National AAU Pentathlon Championship and five consecutive wins in the U.S. National AAU Decathlon Championships. He competed in ten decathlons in 1969, scoring over 8000 points in seven of them. Toomey set a record, with an average of 8321 points in his last three decathlons, a feat that is still unmatched.

Toomey was older than previous decathletes, achieving the 1969 world's record when he was almost 31 years old. During his career, he competed in 38 decathlons, working hard to perform well in each of the events. His strongest performances were in the long jump and the 400-meter race. An injury to his hand in childhood challenged him in the throwing events. Toomey won the championship at the Pan-American Games in 1967, with 8044 points, and held the world's decathlon records in 1966 and 1967.

Toomey has appeared in three films: *Fists of Freedom* (1968); *The World's Greatest Athlete* (1973) and *Summer Games* (1999). He has also worked for all three major networks as a sports commentator and covered the 1972 Olympics for ABC.

Career Achievements

- Toomey won the 1969 Sullivan Award, as the top amateur athlete of the year. In the words of the award, Toomey was judged "by performance and example to have done most to advance the cause of good sportsmanship and amateur athletics."

- He received the Helms World Trophy in 1969.

- The United States Sports Academy presented him with the Distinguished Service Award in 2000.

- He was listed in the 2000 CNN/*Sports Illustrated*'s "50 Top Athletes of the 20th Century" (Connecticut).

- Toomey broke the world record in 1969, in his 10th decathlon of the year and the 38th of his career.

- Toomey set a world's record in the decathlon that lasted for three years.

- He was inducted into the National Track and Field Hall of Fame in 1975.

- Toomey was elected to the U.S. Olympic Hall of Fame in 1984.

- A graduate of the University of Colorado, with a major in journalism, Toomey also earned a masters degree at Stanford.

- He has toured the world for the U.S. State Department with the athletic clinic tour program.

- Toomey was a member of the Presidential Commission on Olympic Sports and the President's Council of Physical Fitness and Sports.

- He served on the Board of Directors of the U.S. Olympic Committee for eight years.

- Toomey helped found the World Olympian Association, whose goals include efforts to increase involvement of Olympians in the education of young people, to promote Olympic ideals, and strengthen the Olympic movement throughout the world.

- Although the exact number of living Olympians is not known, it is estimated that there are slightly more than 60,000.

- Toomey was given the 2000 Distinguished Service Award by the United States Sports Academy.

Bill Toomey (decathlon). (Courtesy the University of Colorado.)

- Toomey was the 1969 *ABC Wide World of Sports* Athlete of the Year.

- He was the 1969 *Field and Track News* Athlete of the Year.

- Toomey was named Alumnus of the Century by the University of Colorado.

Interview

"Sometimes we forget the really important things of life. And to me, the goals and values that were taught to me as a young athlete still hold true—the spirit of keen competition and good sportsmanship."—Bill Toomey

Interviewer's Notes

"Let's jog a lap, Coach," he said.

This was in 1968, at the Lake Tahoe high altitude training camp for the Mexico City Olympic Games.

Bill Toomey ran as slowly as he could without graduating to a walk. At an altitude of 7200 feet, it was all I could do to keep up. He was just fooling around, and I darn near died.

The weather turned cold in August and Bill flew back to the University of Colorado, to work on the pole vault. Some years later I visited with him at Dana Point, California, where he gave me a copy of his book, *The Olympic Challenge* (1984), co-authored with Barry King.

When I asked him to remember his first contact with sports, Toomey recalls his experience with a club on Long Island that had a basketball team.

* * * * *

"I was in the fourth grade," he says, "and my start in sports was running the length of the court without dribbling and throwing it over the backstop! It was in this club that we got discipline, and some tremendous coaching—probably better than kids get today."

"Sports seemed to be more important in those days," he says, "and we had very dedicated people. There are a lot of folks in coaching positions now, but they are not as well-trained. If we screwed up, the coach told us, and we appreciated knowing about it. That doesn't happen anymore.

"Coaches back then played a more expanded role in your physiological and psychological development. Sports seemed to be the only outlet we had. Today's athletes seem more involved in the sea of stimuli outside of sport. There are so many outlets now that many great athletes experience 'burnout.' I call it 'dissipation.'

"If you have a good program," he continues, "there's no such thing as 'burnout.' I resent the term and resist using it, because if something is positive, good and strong, you will continue with it. Only when programs are bad is there the tendency to quit. 'Burnout' is really a bad term—sort of like 'used out.'

"Now 'peaking' is an interesting thing. You can peak five, ten, twenty times a year. It's a matter of preparation—good mental and physical preparation. Competing in the Olympics in October is not the same as competing in the NCAA in the spring. You must have a program that is designed well enough that you can get to the place you want to be. You focus before that happens," Toomey says, but admits "sometimes, you get good performances when you don't know you are ready for them.

"Coaches occasionally use inappropriate programs. I believe that the needs of the athlete must be tailored for a particular time. The coach must really know how to train someone, and know what to share with them that will be helpful. Problems arise when a coach lays out a whole new approach without knowing the background of the individual athlete. Training is a difficult thing, and we don't have that many good books on how to prepare someone. I had to figure out a lot of my training by myself," Toomey says.

"My parents helped me a great deal in my younger days, mostly in the form of support for what I was doing. If I needed a pair of shoes, I knew where I could get them. When parents come to watch practice or competitions, it doesn't interfere with coaching. Positive support is probably the best thing parents can do. My father was great at that.

"There have been obstacles in my career. In my mid-twenties, I was in Germany, confined to bed with mononucleosis and hepatitis. That was a rough time—lying in bed for four months. When I got up, I had to deal with a lot of atrophy. During my illness, there was always the doubt that I would ever compete again. But doubts are only doubts. If you really want something, you can erase them. I won't say it was easy—it was tough. But the positive thing was that I was old enough and smart enough to create a good program.

"My usual competitive weight was about 170 pounds. Later in my career, however, I went up to 195 pounds. This additional weight is all about 'horsepower.' If you have a big engine, you can create more force; a small engine, less force. We used to think that lean and mean was being tough. Actually, it's romping and stomping meat on the hoof that gets the job done.

"I remember J.W. Mashburn from Oklahoma State, a 200-plus quarter miler. He was a character, too. I kind of like characters, as they add a little dimension to the sport. Bland guys don't do much."

Mashburn, inducted into the Oklahoma Hall of Fame in 2001, ran at Oklahoma A&M from 1952 to 1956. A four-time All-American, he ran with the 1600-meter relay team for the Olympic gold in 1956.

When Toomey is asked about coaches he admires, he mentions Ralph Higgins. Higgins, a member of the Track and Field Hall of Fame, was head track coach at OSU for 32 years, where his athletes won 17 straight Missouri Valley Conference team championships. He was later track coach for the U.S. Army track team.

"Ralph was Mashburn's coach at Oklahoma, and he was from the old school," Toomey says, and adds, "There aren't many of those coaches around anymore. Most of the guys now are interested in winning the league or conference. In the old school, coaches worried about the kids in the program. **Berny Wagner,** a past coach at Oregon State, is another terrific guy who comes to mind.

"Pete Peterson may well be the best distance coach in the United States," Toomey says. "If I ever wanted a coach, he would be it. He was a healer, and a trainer—a human being who understood frailties, but knew how to develop strengths. He's the kind of guy we should be developing as coaches. There aren't many of his kind.

"He was a background guy—it was not beneath him to sweep the track or make a pit. He was National coach one year and got a trip to the Los Angeles Coliseum. What a neat guy!" Toomey adds.

"Sports seem to me to be exactly like the business world," he continues. "One of the important parallels is that you can overcome the downside. You know that if you get your act together, there is going to be an upside. I think that's the main thing sport teaches you. Also, A) You can't depend on anyone else; B) there is no such thing as total failure; and C) the future is always available. Sports taught me all of these things.

"I went from the dips to the top of the mountain. I realized it was up to me and that I was in control of my own destiny. An athlete needs to get his resources allocated and not wait for someone to take care of him. You have to do it yourself. If you want to get in shape, no one else can do it for you. No one else is going to be concerned.

"We may believe that vast numbers of people are interested in our successes, but there may be more people who are interested in our failures. Athletes must always be ready for the down times. If you have your mental equipment functioning at a high level, and you've got some resources behind you, you will always make it out of those tough times. Sport is a great teacher for 'upness.' It teaches you that everything is transitory. In sports, as in business, if you make enough right decisions, you will be okay.

"I'd like to mention some ideas about negative thinking," Toomey says. "Whenever you mention something like injuries to another athlete, it's like you are rubbing the wound. I discovered that I had to avoid any kind of negative thoughts or conversations. When you do that, you don't have any negative influences to hinder your performance.

"If you listen to athletes closely, you will hear some whose negativity underlines their entire existence. And where there is doubt, there is a question. It's like when a guy comes up to you and says before a race, 'Are you in shape?' I'm not going to tell him I'm not. I'll say I'm in the greatest shape of my life, and they will follow you right around the track.

"You have to learn how to avoid being negative," he says. "It's a kind of treason, and you don't need that. You have enough doubt, just considering all the dudes out there who are trying to beat your brains out. If you start to beat your own brains out ... well, it's going to be the battle of the midgets. You really can delete a lot of the problems that might hurt your performance by not getting involved with the negative.

"Take animals for example," Toomey says. "They don't think about the negative, just survival, and that's the same thing an athlete has to do. My advice is to be like an animal and work on survival. If you think suicidal, you are on your way to the acorn academy.

"My work with the decathlon has been a tremendous learning experience. The first day of competition is relatively easy—unless you have a ten hour first day. Jenner's first day in Montreal was about four hours. When you tack on an extra six hours plus high jumping in the rain—those kinds of things—it makes it difficult to compare performances."

The 1968 decathlon competition trailed into the evening on both days. More than half of the Olympic Stadium crowd had left the stands when Toomey crossed the finish line of the 1500-meter race to claim the gold.

Beginning in 1932, U.S. decathletes won six consecutive Olympic gold medals. There were no U.S. medal winners at the 1964 Games, which made Toomey's win in 1968 with a score of 8193 all the more welcome. In 1998, a stamp honoring Toomey's performance at the 1968 Olympics was issued by Barbados.

"Every performance is done under different conditions," Toomey says. "In 1948, Bob Mathias threw the discus and shot from a dirt ring. He was a kid who, after his career was over, had done ten decathlons. My number was 38. And how can you compare us with a guy who returned a 95-yard punt from Frank Gifford, for a touchdown? You can't."

Toomey was a high school English teacher at the time of his gold medal win in Mexico City.

"Perhaps tenacity is the most important asset for the decathlon," Toomey says. "Daley Thompson had it."

Thompson, a star decathlete from Great Britain, dominated competition in the decathlon from 1980 to 1987. He won consecutive gold medals at the 1980 and 1984 Games, the second athlete in the history of the modern Games to achieve this feat. (Bob Mathias of the U.S. was first, in 1948 and 1952.) Thompson broke the world's record in 1984, and his score of 8847 remains the Olympic record.

"If you have an injury, it's easy to say, 'I could have done it,' Toomey says. "But I think some of the greatest champions have suffered the most serious injuries. All of the setbacks could not stop the relentless desire.

"I don't know how you get tenacity—it must be a seed that gets planted. Russ Hodge seemed to have injuries that amounted to a plague, but he didn't fail. He was a success—he made the '64 Olympic Team; he was in the Games, and anybody that makes the Olympic Team can never be labeled as a failure."

Hodge set a world record at the Los Angeles Times International Games in 1966 with 8230 points. Between 1963 and 1971, Hodge was ranked first three times, as a member of the U.S. National track and field teams. He placed ninth in the decathlon in the 1964 Tokyo Games.

"I like what **Al Oerter** said about the Olympics," Toomey says. "'You die for them.' We did have an athlete in the Olympics who left his blocks empty. Because of an injury, he was saving himself for another meet.

"I don't understand that stuff—I'm a killer," Toomey says. "Al Oerter is the guy you want leading your platoon. When you are outrageously out-numbered, and you want someone to convince you that you've got a shot, Oerter is the General in the Olympics. I don't know of any athlete who has ever encountered more, or accomplished more.

"At this time, sports seem to be going in the wrong direction. There's too much pressure on the athlete, too many drugs, too much exposure to great amounts of money. At the lower levels of sport, I think we are going in a good direction. We have some people who care about kids—they've been reinvigorated with the knowledge of the importance of the individual.

"Unfortunately, we have a core of elite athletes who are abusers. We have to eradicate that for sports to be important again. There are too many individuals that exhibit sport in ways that imply it should be more than it is. Sport is what an individual makes of it. Sport itself is not evil—it offers opportunity."

Toomey believes that sport should not be singled out, because it really represents the values of society at large. "In my day," Toomey says, "it was easier; we didn't have the temptations and the problems that exist in society today."

As a motivational speaker, Toomey urges young athletes to pair discipline with patience, and to enjoy each part of their training as they work toward their individual performance goals. He urges them to look for the value of each experience and to discover what can be learned from it.

"The elite athletes need to have a shake up," he says. "We have to get these people on track so that the young kids coming up can have someone to respect again. My personal feelings are that young people do not have a lot of respect for the professional athlete. They perceive certain athletes as doing sports for dough—being drugged out or arrested."

"My generation made no money," Toomey says. "We did sports because we wanted to. The feeling is hard to explain. Maybe Avery Brundage was right—who knows? You taint sport with money and you create a whole new need for being better. I think professional sports have demonstrated over the years that a lot of players have abused the privilege of being an athlete. Are they winners? Probably not."

14

Forrest "Spec" Towns

HIGH HURDLES • GOLD MEDAL
Born February 6, 1914, Fitzgerald, Georgia
Died April 9, 1991, Athens, Georgia

Forrest Towns was the first person to break the 14-second mark for the 110-meter hurdles. He won the gold in the hurdles in Berlin in 1936, with a 14.2. Less than a month later, in Norway, Towns ran a 13.7 in the hurdles, an achievement thought to be unattainable at that time. That same year, he won the NCAA and AAU Championships. The record set in Norway was finally authorized by the IAAF in 1938, and remained unbroken for eleven years.

From 1935 to 1937, Towns won more than 60 consecutive races. In 1936 and 1937 he was named to the All-America Outdoor Track and Field Team, and in 1938, he was named to the All-America Indoor Track and Field Team. The first University of Georgia athlete to win a gold medal at the Olympics, Towns served as head track and field coach at Georgia from 1938 to 1975.

Career Achievements

- In 1934, his freshman year, Towns won the Southeastern AAU 120-yard hurdles in 15.1 seconds. The following year as he won the SEC, NCAA, and National AAU titles.

- Towns held the world record of 7.3 seconds in the indoor 60-yard hurdles.

- In 1935 he won the Southeastern Conference title in the 120-yard hurdles with a time of 14.8.

137

- In 1936, Towns was an All-American in the 110-meter hurdles and the 120-yard hurdles.
- He won the NCAA outdoor championship in the 110-meter hurdles.
- Towns also held SEC titles in the 120-yard hurdles with a 14.1, and the 220-yard hurdles in 21.8.
- In 1937, Towns again won the 110-meter and 120-yard hurdles and the NCAA outdoor title in the 120-yard hurdles.
- He earned the SEC Outdoor high point award in 1937, boosting the University of Georgia to their only SEC team title.
- When Towns broke the 14 second mark, he dropped the world record for the 110-meter hurdles by an unprecedented four-tenths of a second.
- Towns equaled the world record of 14.1 for the 110-meter hurdles on five occasions.
- His record 13.7 lasted 11 years, until it was broken by Harrison Dillard, who ran a 13.6 in 1948.
- Towns was inducted into the University of Georgia Athletic Association Circle of Honor, the highest honor given to former Bulldog athletes or coaches.
- In his honor, Georgia currently holds the Spec Towns Invitational every season and also gives an endowment to a track athlete every year.
- Towns was named to the *Track and Field News* Honorable Mention All-Century Team in the 110-meter hurdles, in the March 2000 issue.
- He was inducted in to the State of Georgia Hall of Fame in 1967 and to the United States Track and Field Hall of Fame in 1975.
- Georgia's track and field facility was named for Towns during the 1990 SEC Outdoor Championships.
- Towns was ranked number five among the University of Georgia Athletes of the Century.
- He was ranked among *Sports Illustrated*'s "50 Greatest Georgia Sports Figures." This list of the top 50 greatest 20th-century athletes from each state originally appeared in the Dec. 27, 1999, issue of *Sports Illustrated*.

Forrest Towns (high hurdles) clearing a hurdle. (Courtesy Forrest Towns and the University of Georgia.)

Interview

> *"I was at the finish line when the next runner was coming over the last hurdle."*

Interviewer's Notes

I first met Forrest Towns at the 50th Reunion of the 1936 Olympians. The get-together was held at Ohio State University, Jesse Owens' alma mater. Out of all the men in the crowd, I immediately knew who he was. At 72, he looked like he could still run a good race. Shortly after, we sat down to talk about his experiences as an athlete and his distinguished coaching career.

* * * * *

"As far back as I can remember," Towns begins, "I was always thinking of something to jump. On my grandfather's farm in the summertime, I never went through a gate, I just jumped the fence. I'd watched movies with horses jumping over fences in the steeple chase, and I tried to imitate the horse.

"You know how a horse pulls his front feet back?" he asks. "Well, I would curl my front foot back and drag my back leg, which was perfect hurdler's drag leg, although I didn't know it at the time. When I got to school and started hurdling for real, the coaches had a problem with me, trying to get that front leg straightened out.

"I just loved to jump. When I came home from the park, I would jump all the trash cans that were set on the street. When I was about twelve, I went out in my back yard, put some sticks up and tied a string across them. I put them in the form of a semi-circle, like a horse running on a track. That was the start of being a hurdler, even though I didn't know what I was doing."

Towns graduated from high school in 1931, and went to work, trying a number of different jobs. "I came home from work at the mop factory one day," he remembers, "and found that my younger brother had made some high jump standards. He was in the back yard jumping, so I went back there and jumped with him. I made it as high as the nails went, so my two brothers put the cross bar on their heads. They were both six feet tall, or better. I jumped that with a pair of overalls on.

"There was a newspaper man who lived next door to me, a sports writer. [Tom Wall, who was then the sports editor of the *Augusta Chronicle*.] He happened to be looking out the window, saw me jumping and wrote a small article about it in his sports column. In the article, he suggested that some college was missing a good high jumper.

"The article was shown to the track coach at the University of Georgia" [Weems Baskin, Track and Field Hall of Fame—athlete and coach]. By the time the information got to the coach, I had quit the mop factory and was driving a taxi. The taxi drivers were kind of a rough crowd, and I was right in there with them.

"Coach Baskin came to visit me about going to college. I told him I couldn't, because I had no money. He said I might not need any, and I told him that would be the only way I could go. We made arrangements for me to show up in Athens in September, to see what I could do.

"When I got there, they were just starting football practice. That bunch was the meanest, toughest bunch of people I had ever seen in my life. There I was, 6'2", and weighing just over 150 pounds.

"The track coach and I went to the field house and he asked me if I wanted track shoes with spikes in the heel, as well as the toe. I told him it didn't make much difference because I had never seen a pair. He gave me the track shoes and told me to warm up.

"I had seen other fellows jump and they used the old fashioned scissors style. I figured that was the way you were supposed to jump. My method was to just run straight at it and take off. I had good spring and good speed, so it was just a matter of getting high enough and far enough. Since I was trying out for a track scholarship, I thought I had better scissor.

"When the bar got to 6 feet, I thought it was no time to fool around, so I backed off straight in front of it and curled my front leg up and cleared it. I ended up jumping 6'3". Baskin let me stew for a couple days, and toward the end of the week I told him I had to get back to my job—what goes? That evening he told me I could have room, board, books and tuition for four years!

"Well, I thought, the Depression is on and I'm not making much driving a taxi, and I don't suppose I'll be doing that the rest of my life. If I go to college, the Depression will likely be over in four years, and then I could get a job.

"Coach Baskin had been a hurdler and had held world records in the hurdles. In fact, the first world record I ever broke was his 60-yard indoor. He had been a football player at Auburn University and missed making the 1928 Olympics because he fell in his finals. He came from a long line of hurdle coaches—Wilbur Hutsel had been his coach." (Hutsel was head track coach at Auburn University for 42 years and trained some of the best hurdlers in competition during that time.)

"Wilbur had also worked with another great hurdler, Robert Simpson," Towns says. Simpson, a member of the Track and Field Hall of Fame, was a celebrated hurdler during World War I, setting a world record in 1916 that stood for four years. In 1920, he became head track coach at the University of Missouri, and went on to train some of the finest athletes of the time, including Brutus Hamilton and **Jackson Scholz**.

"They had what was called a double arm action," Towns says, "and spent the majority of their time on technique going over the hurdle. Hurdles in those days were 'T' based. If you hit one of those, it rose up, got between your legs, and you ended up eating cinders.

"The new type are 'L' hurdles. You can often see people winning races even though they knock over three or four hurdles. Well, you didn't hit three or four of the old models! Another old rule was that you could hit two hurdles, but it couldn't be the first one or the last one."

The first time Towns ran on a cinder track, he hit the first hurdle and took a tough fall. But he got up and asked his coach if he could try it again. At this point, his coach said he knew he had a hurdler.

"Coaches looked for a long-legged athlete. Speed was not a major consideration because the first thing you had to do was get over the hurdle. Guys like Harrison Dillard, at 5'10" in height, would have been sent on his way. All the hurdlers before me were not the sprinter type hurdlers.

"It so happened that I had some God-given speed, and my 100-yard time was 9.7. I guess I was the first sprinter type hurdler that came along with long legs. The long legs were important for getting over the hurdles; the speed was something in addition.

"You have hurdlers now who are not as tall, but they have great speed. Renaldo Nehemiah (considered to be the world's finest hurdler between 1978 and 1981; first to run the high hurdles in under 13 seconds) and Gault can run the 100 in 9.3 or 9.4. The emphasis on going over the hurdles is not as great now, as in my time."

Willie Gault's school record time of 7.67 in the 60-meter hurdles at the University of Tennessee, lasted for 20 years.

"The track coaches were all different. Dink Templeton at Stanford had the reputation of being mean and tough." Templeton, a member of the Track and Field Hall of Fame, competed both in field events and rugby (team gold medal) at the 1920 Olympic Games. As a coach, he held practice every day, which was uncommon for that time.

"Then there was Dean Cromwell from Southern California, who was as nice and easy going a fellow as you have ever seen." Cromwell, another Hall of Famer, coached track teams to 12 national collegiate titles. His athletes won 33 national collegiate titles and 38 AOAU championships; set 14 individual world records and 3 relay records; and won 10 Olympic gold medals.

"Brutus Hamilton was the same type. But they were all task masters and demanded discipline. They all had the same basics, and belief in hard work.

"When we got to the Olympics, the coaches didn't try to change us. They were more or less schedulers or facilitators, rather than coaches. They didn't mess with our technique.

"I was never given any instruction in hurdling by Lawson Robinson or any of the other coaches. They respected our coaches and what they had taught us. It would have been very tough for them to take over and demand that we do this or that. No one tried to change me in any way, shape or form, as far as the Olympic coaches were concerned.

"Some people are surprised that I never ran track in high school. As I stated, I came along in high school during the Depression days. My daddy was a railroad man and wasn't working very much. Things were pretty rough with six kids in the family. I was lucky to have a pair of shoes to wear to school, much less buy track shoes. I did play high school football, but they furnished the equipment.

"Nowadays, kids work to support an automobile. So by high school, if there are 1500 students, there will be a thousand cars. In my day, you didn't see a dozen cars around a high school. The University of Georgia has parking space for 50,000 cars, and we have an enrollment of 22,000.

"It is a great thing for school spirit to have athletics. The high schools will be making a great mistake if they cut out physical education and athletics. I have seen reports which show American school children to be the poorest in physical condition of any group of kids in the world. They wouldn't have to be, if we had good programs for physical education in the schools."

Asked to recall his parents involvement in his athletic interests, Towns says, "As long as I did what I was supposed to at home, there was no problem with my folks. I can remember getting into trouble certain times—some of the things I was supposed to do slipped by and didn't get done. When that happened, I got my butt whipped. We had a milk cow and I was supposed to take care of it. It was my job to put her out on grass and give her water.

"My father came home from work about 4:00 one afternoon and that old cow was out there lowing for some water. The bucket was dry and I was in the park playing. I can hear that whistle to this day. I didn't go back to the park for three weeks.

"In those days in Georgia, we were racially separated. The blacks had their school and we had ours. We also had our own playground. In that situation, we never competed with each other. That was a shame, as far as I'm concerned. I gave the first scholarship to a black athlete at the University of Georgia.

"Now, of course, it is completely integrated all the way down to grammar school. Even though black schools had their programs, and we had ours, I'm sure they didn't have as many advantages, because they didn't have as much money. The first time I competed against black athletes was in the National Collegiate track meets.

"After the 1936 Olympics, representatives of different countries, in league with the Americans, set up meets all over the world. I agreed to go to Norway and Sweden. Before that, we had a meet in Hamburg, Germany, and then a duel meet in London against the British Empire. From there it was Stockholm and back to Paris for a triangular meet involving France, Japan, and the United States. We then went to Oslo, Norway, and on to Sweden for two or three more meets, competing until late September. I would say they got their money's worth out of us.

"The AAU had a rule that if you entered a track meet and it was advertised that you were going to be there, they could rule you ineligible for a period of sixteen months if you didn't show up for any reason other than sickness or death in your family. A funny thing happened when I was in Paris. I got a telegram from my football coach, which I viewed as kind of a joke, although I was still interested in playing football. In the telegram he told me that the 'minor' sports season was over, that the football season started September 1, and for me to be there. I had a chance to make the Georgia team that year, so it was important to me.

"I went to Dan Ferris, the secretary/treasurer of the AAU, who made the travel arrangements, and asked him for a release. I was an obstinate person and got upset about the rules. I ran into **Glenn Cunningham**, who was an old timer and knew the rules. It was from him that I heard about the sixteen month suspension from the AAU. That penalty would have taken care of my senior year.

"So, everything considered, I went to Oslo, even though I wasn't in the best frame of mind. That was where I set the World Record of 13.7 in the high hurdles. When I say the record was set there, you will have to realize it was a unique situation, as far as recognizing world records. The IAAF are the only people who can authorize a new record. This group meets every two years. We were in an Olympic year so they had already met and passed on all the records, including those of the Olympic Games.

"They had passed on my 14.1, which was an Olympic and World's Record. I ran 14.1 eleven times. When I ran this 13.7, it was phenomenal, since it was the first time anyone had run under 14 seconds in the high hurdles. I guess it seemed unbelievable, so they didn't pay much attention to it. Perhaps it was the wind, or something of that sort.

"When the officials met again in 1938, the IAAF had applications for the world records from Layberth of South Africa for 14.0. It happened that Layberth was in the 13.7 race in Norway. Of course, the people in Norway started pushing the application for my world record, as it would be a feather in their cap it if was run in their country.

"The record application was passed, and it is my understanding there was a movie which showed me winning the race by 15 yards. I was at the finish line when the next runner was coming over the last hurdle. It was a phenomenal race, as far as I was concerned. I did have the best start I had ever had, the track was extremely fast, and it was just a good day, except for me being a little peeved about having to go to the meet. So the 13.7 was accepted as a World Record in 1938, and it stood until 1950, when Dick Attelsey from Southern California broke it."

Reflecting on the state of values in the country and among athletes, Towns says, "It scares me to think what will happen to my grandchildren.

Values today don't seem to show right and wrong as when I was growing up. Nobody had to tell me to do this or that; I knew what was wrong because of my upbringing. It is a great concern to me what will happen to this world if it continues as it is.

"Go back to the original Olympics and study the history of it," Towns says. "A man who won a gold medal in the original Olympic Games never had to work another day in his life. He was a hero. The Games now have gotten completely out of hand, as far as amateurs are concerned. I still think there can be a plan for an athlete who competes, more than just the pleasure of it.

"Nowadays, schools have to pay more and more for their athletes. When I went to school, tuition was $42.50 per quarter. Back in the '50s, it seemed unimaginable that our budget for athletics would reach $500,000. The athletic budget is now in excess of several million.

"When I started at the University, I asked the track coach if I could play football, and he said it was okay. You see, he was a football coach too; track was just a sideline with him. I made the freshman team and they red shirted me my sophomore year. Football was also important to the Towns family: Towns lettered as a substitute end on the Georgia football team in 1936 and 1937. His son, Bobby, lettered in football and track at Georgia (1957–59), and played for the St. Louis Cardinals in the National Football League from 1960 to 1963. Towns' grandson, Kirby, was the third generation to letter in football and track at the University of Georgia (1996–98). He set state track records his senior year in the 110-meter and 300-meter hurdles. "I graduated in 1937 and the head coach, Harry Mare, said, 'If you come back and play that year, I'll put you on the coaching staff.'

"That's where I stayed; I have never been anywhere else except during the war years. [Towns spent four years in the U.S. Army, serving in Europe and Africa.] I held the head track job from 1938 until I retired in 1975.

"Sports have been my life. It is really all I have done since 1933, when I entered the University of Georgia. Sports was it. At the beginning, I didn't have any idea of being a track coach. When I went to Georgia, I had no idea what I would do when the four years were up.

"One important thing I learned from sports was how to discipline my life. There were also some valuable lessons for getting along with others. During my first few years, I started developing ways to help young people. I got a lot out of life from the athletes I helped coach. I still get telephone calls from out of the blue.

"I'm sure I was a tough coach, and the boys will tell you that. Discipline to me was a big thing. It makes me feel good when they come back and say how much I did for them. Sometimes, you write off a boy and years later they come back and tell you what they've accomplished."

As a coach, he watched films of athletes from around the world, and passed on what he learned to his athletes. During his tenure at Georgia, his athletes won five individual SEC titles and 21 individual outdoor titles.

"There have been so many things that have been enjoyable to me in sports, that it would be tough to pick out a real high point," Towns says. "The track stuff was more or less ordinary to me. It was just something I loved to do. Anything that you do well doesn't seem to be that important.

"But I do remember one occasion that stands out," Towns says. "In the Southeast Conference, Louisiana State University had been the big wheel in track and field, since the organization of the conference in 1931. In my senior year, we won the Southeast Conference, which was a big surprise to everybody. On that particular day, I was a high point man by winning both the high and low hurdles, second in the high jump, and third in the 100-yard dash."

LSU, the defending champion, with 50+ athletes, would seem to have had the edge over the Bulldog team of 15 men. But Towns earned high point honors with 16.5, and led Georgia to the 1937 SEC Team Championship, their only track and field SEC title.

15

Craig Virgin

LONG DISTANCE RUNNING • THREE TIME
OLYMPIC FINALIST IN THE 10,000 METER RACE
Born August 2, 1955, Belleville, Illinois

An accomplished road and track runner, Craig Virgin was rated national or world class for most of his 23-year career. A nine-time All-American, Virgin made the U.S. Olympic track and field team in the 10,000-meter event three times, while battling a serious, life-long chronic illness. He was the first runner to break both the high school, collegiate, and U.S. National records of America's premier runner, Steve Prefontaine.

In 1979, Virgin ran the 10,000-meter race in 27:39.4, at the Mt. SAC Relays, taking 4.2 seconds off Prefontaine's U.S. record 27:43.6 run in 1974. In July of 1980, he ran the 10,000 in 27:29.16, taking 10 more seconds from his own record, at the Sport 2000 meet in Paris.

Because of the U.S. boycott of the Olympic Games in 1980, Virgin did not get the chance to compete in Moscow, but would have been favored to be the first American since Billy Mills (Tokyo, 1964) to win a medal in the event. Virgin qualified for the 1976 Olympic team, but did not make the final. He ran his first marathon in 1979 in San Diego, and won the race in 2:14.40, the fastest time recorded for a first time racer in the event. During his career, Virgin was twice ranked second in the world in the 10,000 meters.

Virgin won the IAAF Long Course Individual World Cross-Country Championship in Paris in 1980, the first and only American to do so, then and now, with a time of 37:01. He won again at Madrid in 1981, with a 35.05. He retired from national and international competitive running in January of 1992.

147

Craig Virgin (long distance running) at the head ("USA") of a group of runners. (Courtesy Craig Virgin.)

Career Achievements

- Virgin was two-time IAAF World Cross Country Champion. He qualified for ten U.S. International Cross Country teams, beginning in 1978.

- He was three-time U.S. Track and Field Olympian in the 10,000 meters, placing first in 1980 and second in 1976 and 1984.

- Virgin was the first American male to qualify for three consecutive Olympic teams in the 10,000 meters.

- He ran the fastest time in the world for 10,000 meters (27:29.2) just two weeks before the 1980 Olympics, but was unable to compete because of the U.S. boycott of the Games.

- Virgin was on the Atlanta Committee for the Olympic Games, which brought the 1996 event to the city.

- He was a silver medalist in the 10,000-meter event at the 1979 World Cup Track Meet in Montreal.

- Virgin was ranked second in the World in the 10,000-meter event by *Track and Field News* in 1979 and 1980.

- He won the Olympic Sports Festival 5,000-meter event in 1981.

- Virgin was the winner of many premiere non-marathon road races in the U.S., including: Maggie Valley 8K Moonlight Run, Peachtree 10K Road Race, Crescent City 10K Classic, Bermuda 10K International Road Race, Red Lobster 15K Classic, Bay to Breakers 12K Road Race, Falmouth 12K Road Race, Tevira Twosome Ten-Mile Race.

- In high school, Virgin was selected as *Track and Field News* prestigious High School Athlete of the Year in 1973.

- He was National AAU Junior Champion at the three-mile distance in 1973, and the National High School record holder in the two-mile distance.

- Virgin won five Illinois High School State Championships: the 1972 and 1973 Cross Country, two mile and one mile.

- He still holds the course record at the Illinois State three-mile Cross Country Championship course in Peoria, Illinois, and the two mile record at the Illinois State High School Track Championships.

- Virgin set nine national age group records at distances from 3,000 to 5,000 meters during high school.

- He set four national high school grade level records at two-mile distances.

- Virgin is the former U.S. Collegiate record holder for the 10,000-meter run, with 27:59.4, set in 1976.

- He won the NCAA Cross Country Championship in 1975 at Penn State.

- Virgin won 13 championships in Illinois Intercollegiates. He was nine-time NCAA All-American and nine-time Big Ten Champion in cross country, indoor track and outdoor track.

- He was named to the U.S. National Distance Running Hall of Fame at Utica, New York in 2001.

- Virgin is the president and founder of *Front Runner Inc.*, a sports marketing and promotion company. He also does freelance radio and television broadcast work and public speaking.

Interview

"Before someone else can beat you, you have to give up."

Interviewer's Notes

In the town of Lebanon, Illinois—population 3500—almost everyone knew Craig Virgin. For many years, I would look out the window in all kinds of weather, to see a solitary runner, light of step, passing by. His daily runs were side-lined with waves and encouraging remarks. Sometimes, by chance, I would drive alongside him, for a quick conversation.

Craig's high school coach, Hank Feldt, was a well-respected coach and teacher in the area, and was a key contributor to the early development of this premiere runner.

* * * * *

When I ask Craig when he was first aware of sports, he says "somewhere between kindergarten and second grade, in physical education classes. Then," he adds, "I discovered the Cardinals! One of my early memories was getting a transistor radio and being able to listen to baseball broadcaster Harry Carey, with Jack Buck as his understudy.

"My first love in those days was baseball," Virgin says. "I was a pretty good player, mostly at short stop and second base. In grade school, my dream was to someday be a second baseman or short stop for the St. Louis Cardinals.

"I loved to read, and I began to check out books about athletes and athletics from the school library. The typical plot in these books involved a local town athlete who was good in sports and had a chance to win a scholarship to the state university. When you live out in the country and ride the school bus, you have a lot of time to read. I was enthralled with these sports books and I loved playing sports. Kids older than me often invited me to play with them.

"My eighth grade basketball coach believed in pre-season conditioning, and because I was a very mediocre basketball player, I figured the only way I could stay on the team was to out-hustle the other players. Running in the drills was what caught the attention of the coach, and he suggested that I might want to go out for cross country.

"My dad is a farmer. He didn't go to college, but he did participate in track and field in high school. When my grandfather found out that he was having trouble with a knee injury, he told Dad to stay home and help milk the cows. They didn't have much sports medicine in those days."

Asked what his parents contributed to his development, Virgin says, "I inherited mental toughness from my mother, and physical endurance from my dad—the ability to adapt to the environment and work in all kinds of weather. My folks were the two most influential role models in my life.

"When I was a child on the farm, it was a very physical, vigorous environment. Doing manual labor, despite bad conditions, develops toughness—both physically and mentally—and I learned to tolerate physical discomfort. Certain farm work had to be done, regardless of the weather, much like what it takes to be a successful distance runner. This is one of the reasons I call myself a 'white Kenyan,' because of the physically rigorous childhood I experienced, compared to most American boys today."

Virgin credits his life on a farm near Lebanon, Illinois, with providing a place to develop his running skills. The long and rolling country roads that reached out in all directions from his family's home gave him an ideal practice venue. He believes that he would not have become as good a runner had he grown up in a city or a sprawling suburban setting.

"At the age of five," Virgin says, "I was plagued with constant urinary tract infections, and was hit by most of the childhood diseases within a span of twelve weeks in kindergarten. The doctors at Cardinal Glennon Children's Hospital in St. Louis told my parents that I would probably not live into my teens. I survived on oral and intravenous antibiotics for the next eight years.

"But during this time," he adds, "I learned to focus on my body—to monitor my physical symptoms and manage my disease. I also learned how to tune out pain and discomfort. You can't disregard it totally—you have to acknowledge it—but I developed the ability to compartmentalize it and push it to the edge of my consciousness, so it wouldn't overwhelm me."

Virgin believes that the frequent times he spent in the hospital made him mentally tough. "I realized that you can't beat nature," he says, "but you can fool her for a little bit. In distance running, you have to admit that you will eventually become exhausted. But it's necessary to run as fast and far as you can, putting off the inevitable as long as possible. I listened to my body during training and races, and tried to become more efficient—to get the most results from any given energy.

"Things went from bad to worse in the eighth grade," Virgin remembers. "I underwent reconstructive bladder surgery in November of 1968. As part of the reconstructive process, I had to have my bladder drained externally to a leg bag for eight weeks. Here I was in the eighth grade— 13 years old and already self-conscious—and I had to wear that leg bag for a couple of months. It didn't make me feel very attractive to girls, believe me! But I kept focusing on my goal, which was to beat the disease. Two months later, I got my reward when I had the catheter and leg bag removed, and was pronounced healthy again by the doctors."

Virgin says that stories about athletes who persevered in the face of physical challenges inspired him. "I read about **Glenn Cunningham**," he says, "and how no one thought he would ever walk again. But after being seriously burned as a child, he became the world record holder in the mile. Wilma Rudolph had polio and wore braces in grade school. When they finally removed the braces in high school, she became one of the greatest female athletes of all time.

"Athletes like Cunningham and Rudolph worked hard to overcome these challenges and theirs were the stories I read as a kid. They had a great deal of influence on me, which in turn led me to hope that I could overcome my problems some day. Athletic participation gave me the foundation to build my self-confidence and self-esteem.

"From 1978 to 1982, I was in my prime as a runner. I was two-time World Cross Country Champion and the American record holder at 10,000 meters. I believe that I could have been a true Olympic medal contender if the American team had participated in the 1980 Games. I caught a virus in the Olympic village in 1976, and did not make the finals. In 1984, I was bothered by knee problems.

"My goal in 1980," Virgin says, "was to be the first American since Billy Mills (1964, Tokyo) to win a medal in the 10,000 meters. In March, we had the World Cross-Country Championships in Paris. I came from behind, in a dramatic sprint, to beat a good field that day.

"At the time, there was already talk about a potential boycott of the Moscow Olympics by the U.S. and other allied countries. I had done a research paper at the University of Illinois on the Olympics and knew about the ancient Games in Greece, as well as the history of the event from the time it was revived in 1896. Other attempts to use a boycott at the Games as a political maneuver had not been successful.

"For example, in Montreal in 1976, the African coalition wanted the IOC (International Olympic Committee) to punish the New Zealand Olympic Team because it had allowed a South African soccer team to play. Avery Brundage declined. The African countries packed their bags and walked out, two days before opening ceremonies. I saw the damage that did. It really didn't stop apartheid, but there we were, four years later, considering a U.S. boycott of the Olympics, because of the USSR invasion of Afghanistan.

"I was against the boycott and got some heat for saying so. Some people thought it was self-serving for me to state my opposition, but the boycott went against the grain of what I thought the Olympics were supposed to be."

Virgin believes that the true purpose and value of the Games is to bring people together from all over the world under the Olympic banner—to celebrate the commonalities they have through sports and training—as opposed to focusing on the differences. "Sport is the true international language," he says. "The Olympic Games work best when they about inclusion, rather than exclusion.

"I had prepared physically and mentally for the 1980 Games and was ready," he continues. "Even at the trials, I still had hopes for the Games. I made the team and set the Olympic trials record that year. Ten days before the Games were to begin, I ran the year's fastest 10,000 meters, and set a new American record. I also ran the fastest 5000-meter race ever run in Europe, two times that month.

"It was a great disappointment not to go, but there are some things in life that you cannot control. I had to accept it and go on. I still wonder what would have happened, if I had faced the Ethiopian, Miruts Yifter, again in the 10,000-meter final.

"The Games would be coming up again in 1984, and I told myself that I'd be in even better shape. I'd be a little older and should have a world's record by then. That's what I decided to focus on.

"But I started having physical problems and was not a medal contender by 1984. I'd been very intense with my training and competition from early on, but unfortunately, an athlete is only one injury away from being run of the mill. The difference between being great and just good is sometimes very small.

"Through the years, I've had many friends among my competitors. There was one distance runner, Robby Perkins, from a Virginia high school, and we ran against each other—on paper. He would run fast times out there, and I would try to beat them, back in the Midwest. There was another guy from New York, Matt Cerntrowitz, who also ran fast times back in the early '70s.

"Matt went on to make two Olympic teams," Virgin says. "Robbie never made the team, but he competed in many national championships over the years."

Virgin remembers another runner, Terry Williams, from California, who was one of three runners in high school that he ran against in college and the NCAA Championships.

"I was lucky when I won nine Big Ten titles," he says, "because I ran against some really tough competition. Greg Meyer, from Michigan, who went on to win the Boston Marathon, was one of the better runners in history. Another Wolverine, Bill Donokowski, won several major road races and marathons after college.

"Herb Lindsey was one of the runners I respected most in college. He ran for Michigan State and won several Big Ten titles. He became one of my rivals, from 1980 to 1984. There was also another Spartan, Stan Mavis, who set a half-marathon American record.

"The runner that I ran against in both collegiate and international competition was Nick Rose. We were fierce competitors when Nick was at Western Kentucky [Rose was a native of Bristol, England] and I was at the University of Illinois. He was one of the runners I respected most, throughout my athletic career."

He added, "Yifter from Ethiopia was a tremendous competitor—he won golds in the five and the ten." Miruts Yifter, nicknamed "Yifter the Shifter" was the talented Ethiopian runner whose trademark was his ability to sprint away from a pack of runners during the final 400 meters of a race.

"My African role model," Virgin says, "was Kip Keino." Hezekiah Kipchoge Keino, a Kenyan distance runner, won four Olympic medals—

gold in the 1500 and silver in the 5000 meters in 1968; gold in the 3000-meter steeplechase and silver in the 1500 meters in 1972.

Virgin "was impressed when Abebe Bikila won the Marathon in Rome, running barefoot." Bikila was the first man to win consecutive Olympic marathons, in 1960 and 1964.

"My American heroes at that time were Steve Prefontaine, Frank Shorter, Bill Rogers and Marty Liquori," Virgin says. "If you asked me who is or was the greatest distance runner, I couldn't say, because each has his own claim to fame. Shorter won a gold and silver medal in the marathon in 1972 and 1976. Rogers won four New York City and Boston marathons, but never qualified for an Olympic team. Marty Liquori (the third high school runner—of four—to break the four minute mile) was an American record holder at a couple of the distances, but only made one Olympic team.

"Prefontaine owned most of our American distance records," Virgin says, "from the 2000-meter to the 10,000-meter race. Yet he never won an Olympic medal, a world championship or a major road race."

Prefontaine, elected to the Track and Field Hall of Fame in 1991, is considered to have been one of America's greatest distance runners, ever. Winner of two AAU titles and six national collegiate titles, Prefontaine's career ended prematurely with a fatal car crash in 1975.

"I was never an Olympic medalist or owned a world record," Virgin says, "but I did win the World Cross Country Championship twice. And at this time (2004), I still have the records for the Olympic trials in the 10,000 meters and the U.S. Championship 10,000 meters, which have stood for over 20 years.

"The best you can ever hope for," Virgin says, "is to be lumped in with the top guys. It is disrespectful to say that one person is better than the rest. You can refer to a top handful of people."

When asked about a particularly memorable race in his career, Virgin says, "In 1978, the World Cross Country Championships were in Glasgow, Scotland. As a rookie, I finished sixth. In 1979, the race was in Limerick [Ireland], and I was shooting for the top three. I was stuck in the mud, back about 120th, and just ran my little butt off to get up to 13th place. I passed and passed the other runners, until I got to the finish line. So I ran harder in 1979 to finish 13th, than I did the year before to finish sixth!"

Competitive cross country running began as a game in England in the early 1800s. Runners dropped pieces of paper or other markers in a random trail for other runners to follow. Called "the paper chase" or "hare and hounds," the first formal competition was held at Rugby School in

1837, and soon became a popular game at other schools throughout England. Hare and hounds gained popularity at Oxford and Cambridge universities, where the chase became a cross-country race, and the course was laid out in advance.

There was not an official world championship in Cross Country until 1973, when the IAAF declared an official World Championship. The winner of the International Cross of Nations, begun in 1903 in Scotland, had previously been considered to be equivalent to this title, and the winners were usually either British or French.

Virgin continued, "In 1980, I won our trials easily. I had been second in the 1979 World Cup 10,000 meters, when Yifter beat me. I thought I could finish in the top three. I was also the team captain that year.

"We had a false start," Virgin remembers. "I was organizing my teammates in the box, which was very narrow, and was trying to get them two abreast, which wasn't working out very well. They shot off the starting gun with my back to the field. I almost got run over by my own teammates! I ended up pivoting and cursing and tried to get through the crowd.

"At the kilometer mark, I was probably 69th. Runners were in front and I couldn't pass. All I could do was either give up—or keep hanging in there, and fight and hope that I could get a chance to move up.

"Finally, there was an opening. I squeezed through and passed three or four guys. At the four or five kilometers mark of a 12 kilometer race, I was in the top 25; and with two laps to go—about four miles into the race, I caught the back of the lead pack.

"Then I discovered that 60–70 yards out front of the lead pack of three or four runners, was Nick Rose, from England. What should I do? Should I stay there in the security of this pack and cruise along? Or should I set sail—take a big chance, go out in no-man's land—and try to chase him down?"

"You take a risk when you do that," Virgin says, "and you look really dumb if you fail. But I told myself that I didn't come 3,000 miles from Lebanon, Illinois, to take the easy way out. So I slingshot around that pack and set sail for Rose. My goal was to be on his shoulder by the time of the bell lap. Then I would try to out sprint him in the end.

"I tried my best," Virgin remembers. "I closed from 70 yards to ten yards, and with a lap to go, he looked behind and put on a spurt. I lost my momentum and at that point was no longer battling for first. I was trying my best to hold on to second place.

"Third and fourth were coming up alongside of me. Again, I had a tough decision to make. Do I quit or continue the fight? I was out of gas—I could quit—I'd given it the old college try. Or I could fight...

"I chose to fight. I had come this far, and it's not over until the fat lady sings, or you cross the finish line. So I fought off third or fourth place. Although Rose had gotten away from us, trying to hold the other guys off got me close enough again to challenge. In the last 600 yards of the race, a West German went by me, but I thought he had started his sprint too soon.

"There was a 600-yard final straightaway in front of the grandstand. I had these little visual cues (landmarks I'd set up before the race) that told me when to change gears. I decided to stick to my original plan.

"The West German started to run down Rose, and got by him with 200 yards to go. He then took the lead by five or six yards. Finally, with about 150 yards to go, I got past Rose, and in the last 20 yards, I passed the West German to finally win it!

"It was a very exciting finish," Virgin says, "the closest thing to the Billy Mills 10,000-meter race in 1964. Gammoudi [Mohamed Gammoudi of Tunisia] and Ron Clarke [Australian and world's multi-record holder] were fighting it out, when Mills slipped by both of them, to claim America's only gold medal ever in the 10,000 meters.

"I won the World's Championship again the next year, over an Ethiopian, and again in the last hundred yards. I didn't give up in the race, although there were four or five times when I could have," he says. "Both victories were momentous breakthroughs for me. Before someone else can beat you, you have to give up. You have to allow yourself to be beaten."

Asked about current training methods for distance runners, Virgin says, "I don't think the basics have changed much from the '70s or '80s." Virgin's training in school spanned the period of time from 1969 until 1977, when he was a high school and college student. In his prime running years, Virgin ran 90–105 miles a week, along with weight training and flexibility work. (He also attended classes or worked a regular schedule.)

"I helped pioneer 'Athletics West' in 1977–78", he continues. "It was the first Nike sponsored team, during their early days. That summer, I traveled to Europe and spent three months competing and visiting with European athletes and coaches. When I came home to Lebanon, Illinois, my training was pretty well solidified. That fall, I wrote a thesis on how to do an eleven-month U.S. training program, designed to match the European schedule.

"When I look back and reflect, one of the popular training methods for distances runners in the late 1960s and early 1970s was called LSD—Long, Slow, Distance. During this time, it was outstanding for an American miler to break four minutes. Previously, many of the coaches were too focused on interval speed training. There was not enough base work. Certainly in the late '60s and early '70s, training was out of balance. Long, slow, distance training ultimately produces long, slow distance runners.

"By the late '70s and early '80s, we were back in balance. Distance runners were doing 90 to 120 miles per week, incorporating 2–3 speed days a week. The rest was over-distance work. The speed days were used to prepare the body for anaerobic work. The distance training built up aerobic endurance.

"One thing that gave Nike a leg up over their competitors was that manufacturers were slow to pick up the fact that most of the distance running for Americans was on sidewalks and roads. In Germany, there are a great many parks with trails, but in the United States, there is no understanding of that. If we tried to run on golf courses, we were chased off—even most Olympians.

"Unfortunately for Americans, they don't often have a choice. Certainly, we have some wonderful indoor and outdoor tracks, and in Kenya, they don't even have that. They do, however, have miles and miles of dirt roads."

When Virgin is asked if the Olympiads should be held in Greece, he says, "I have not been to Athens in recent years, but when I was there, the Athens airport was one of the least secure. From a romantic stand-point, it would be a great idea. Realistically, it is probably a bad idea. During the time of the summer Olympics, Athens is very hot, and 15–20,000 athletes (not to mention 250,000+ spectators) descending on the city every four years would pose a problem with housing and transportation."

Virgin proposes an alternative: "We could have four to six sites around the world that could become host sites, and the Games would rotate among them. The Olympics are getting so expensive that most cities cannot afford to build the infra-structure from scratch, and raise the amount of money they need to do so.

"I believe that between the Israeli athlete massacre in 1972 and the Montreal financial disaster of 1976, the IOC movement was in grave danger. Moscow was going to have the Games in 1980, come hell or high water. You knew the money, if needed, would come from their national treasury.

"Many regarded the Olympics as too expensive, too unwieldy, and a security nightmare. When Los Angeles got the Olympics in 1984, they didn't have much competition. Peter Ueberroth, using good old-fashioned marketing skills and American capitalism, created a business template where the Olympics would not just break even financially, but could also make a profit, under the right conditions.

"With as much money as the IOC is now making, they need to do more funding in third world countries, for facilities and equipment. Then there are our own American athletes who are struggling, and receive little help.

"Because of the money that can now be made in international track and field, coaches and performance-enhancing drug experts are hired by agents, who stand to make a percentage of the athlete's winnings. This is true with distance runners, as well."

Virgin believes that the use of professional athletes in Olympic competitions has swung the pendulum too far away from the original intent of the Games.

"It was a national pride thing," he says, "and it involved the way we were going about selecting our U.S. basketball team. I believe, for example, that we could have fielded an all-star collegiate team in basketball that would have done very well. The rest of the world was catching up to us, however, because basketball had become an international sport. We decided to create the 'Dream Team,' with the best of the NBA players involved.

"It was like a 600 pound gorilla entering the tournament. There wasn't much competition, although it was good for American morale. Americans love to win and win big. And because basketball was invented in the U.S., we think we own it. We went duck hunting with a cannon.

"Some of the pros took it easy in the last Olympiad or two. It was a sacrifice for them financially and physically, but they stayed in deluxe hotel suites, while most other Olympic team members were in the dorm rooms in the Olympic Village.

"The same situation developed with the American hockey team. But that first team did not do very well, and they ended up trashing their living quarters. It was a real embarrassment to the United States Olympic Committee and the country.

"Most of us have a romantic vision of the Olympics being a pure and honest form of competition. It is supposed to be an extension of the ancient Olympic Games, in which truces were called in wars, and athletes were given time off to train. Instead of killing each other, they competed for honor and pride.

"De Coubertin tried to reclaim this," Virgin says, "and he was successful, except for the fact that the Games were shackled by the amateur chain. (In 1894, Baron Pierre de Coubertin, a French educator, proposed the revival of the Olympic Games on an international scale.) Avery Brundage was very big in this. What he made of the Olympics in the early to mid–20th century was a 'blue blood' sport. Only certain financially well-off members of the population could afford to be an Olympian.

"There have been politics involved in the Olympics since the modern games began in 1896. If you know where to look and what doors to open, the undue influence of politics is there. None of what happens should surprise us. Athletes, for years, were held back from making a living from their sport—even a modest one. Those athletes either had to take a vow of poverty to train and compete, or they had to be financially independent.

"It's my belief that the Olympics changed massively from 1972 on. Television and marketing brought about national and international exposure. The cost of the Olympics now isn't just the cost of the infrastructure. Hotels and public transportation are a major consideration. In Atlanta, there were 15,000 to 18,000 athletes and officials—and 22,000 additional security personnel!

"The IOC should establish levels of decorum, not only for athletes, but also the countries they represent, and of course, the media. I doubt that we will ever be able to get politics out of the equation. But guidelines are needed, so that politics do not obstruct the Olympic movement and the Olympic ideals—ideals that the world still needs in the present as much as they did in 1896."

After being sidelined by knee problems that prevented him from qualifying for the 1988 Olympics, Virgin came back in 1990 to win a cross country invitational race at the University of Illinois, 12 years after his graduation. Virgin also learned to cross-train to prepare for running, using a combination of weightlifting, swimming and stationary bike workouts.

In 1997, Virgin fought to recover from a near-fatal automobile accident. Eleven operations, physical therapy and two years later, Virgin returned to running.

16

Carl B. "Berny" Wagner

COACH
Born 1924, Fresno, California

Twice named an Olympic coach, Berny Wagner gained fame as head coach at Oregon State University (1965–1975), where he coached 25 NCAA Division I All-American athletes, in 12 different events. He developed four Olympians, including **Dick Fosbury,** gold medalist at the 1968 Games in Mexico City.

Wagner coached ten open national and national collegiate champions (four in the high jump). At the 1975 Pan American Games, Wagner coached two gold medal jumpers—Joni Huntley and Tom Woods.

At Oregon State, Wagner designed and developed Patrick Wayne Valley Field, which served as the track and field stadium for the university from 1974 to 1988, when the program at OSU was dropped for financial reasons.

From 1978 to 1981, Wagner served as the first executive director of TFA/USA (Track and Field Association of the USA), a merger between the United States Track and Field Association and the United States Track Coaches Association. Wagner was Technical Advisor for Athletics for the San Diego Olympic Training Center Foundation, and was National Coach/Coordinator for the Athletics Congress from 1981 to 1989.

Career Achievements

- In 2002, Wagner was inducted into the United States Track Coaches Association National Hall of Fame.
- Wagner was inducted into the Oregon State Hall of Fame for his ten years of winning teams in Track and Field.

Berny Wagner (coach). (Courtesy Berny Wagner.)

- Wagner was inducted into the San Mateo County Sports Hall of Fame for his ten years at the high school and college, where his teams won conference championships, had several undefeated seasons and an undefeated streak of 83 consecutive wins in high school meets.

- Berny Wagner was inducted into the city of Lodi Sports Hall of Fame, along with his 1954 varsity track and field team. That year, the team won the SAC–Joaquin Conference Championship, the only conference title the school has ever won in track and field. (Wagner notes that Lodi was a good football, basketball and baseball town.)

- Wagner has served as volunteer coach of men's and women's high jumpers at Western Oregon State /Western Oregon University for 14 years, producing 15 NAIA high jump All-Americans, a three-time National Champion and his eighth seven-foot-plus jumper.

- During Berny Wagner's tenure as OSU, his track and field teams had a 49–24 record in dual meets.

- Wagner's teams finished in the top 20 of the NCAA Championships 16 times, and finished in the top six four times.

- Wagner was a member of the U.S. Men's Track and Field Olympic Committee and the NCAA Track and Field Rules committee.

- He was chair of the Pacific Association of the AAU Men's Track and Field Committee and President of the California Track and Field Association.

- He was starter at the 1962 USA/USSR Dual Meet, and served as a referee for NCAA track and cross country championships.

- At San Mateo College, where Wagner was head track, field and cross-country coach from 1962 to 1965, he developed curricula for and taught two experimental courses in isometrics and weight training.

- His teams won the Conference championship in 1964 and 1965, and the West Coast Relays Championship in 1964.

- The San Mateo cross country teams were 25–1 and won the Conference Championship in 1963 and 1964.

- Wagner was Men's Head Coach of the 1992 USA Indoor Track and Field Team vs. Great Britain.

- He has had articles published in *Scholastic Coach, Track and Field News, The Oregon Journal, U.S. Track Coaches Association Quarterly, Journal of the Division of Girls' and Women's Sports,* and *Olympic Track and Field Techniques.*

- Wagner wrote articles for the IAAF's advanced technique book *Athletes in Action* on subjects that include isometrics, high jumping, coed methods classes, the Olympic Games and starting.

Tips from the Coach

Wagner believes that the art of coaching is "leading people and nurturing greatness in others. Coaches who listen to their athletes and allow them to share in decision- making are in partnership with their athletes."

According to Wagner, it is the coach's job to provide leadership, guidance and direction to achieve the desired objective, but athletes must set their own goals and work toward them.

"Some people think the partnership style of coaching means that the coach lets the athletes do anything they want … this is not the case. This is the most difficult and time-consuming kind of coaching, but it is best for the athletes' development and competitive performance. You really have to want to coach to take this route," Wagner says.

According to Wagner, a good coach should have a well-thought-out reason for everything they do in coaching, be willing to revise their thinking, and not accept mediocrity in any form. Attention to detail is critical, and is "the foundation upon which consistency is built," he says.

"The coach must have genuine respect for the young people they are working with, show respect to them and aspects of their lives other than athletics. Respect can't be demanded or dictated; it must be earned.

"A good coach learns from athletes … and realizes that there are different ways of achieving effective techniques and results. They must remember that each athlete is different from others."

Wagner urges coaches to be "people-centered" and not technique or event-centered. "Praise good points, even in a disastrous performance," he says. "There is always something good, even in a failure."

Wagner believes that athletes must be responsible for their own actions—punctuality on team trips, team meetings and workouts; practice and competition gear, when needed. He also believes that "the event must belong to the athlete, not the coach. When an athlete achieves a personal record or other good performance, the credit goes to them, and to no one else.

"After working with a good coach for three years," Wagner concludes, "an athlete should be able to coach themselves and help others."

Interview

"The things that mean the most to me are not documented. They are comments or letters from former high school and college athletes."

Interviewer's Notes

I first became acquainted with Berny Wagner when we shared quarters during the 1968 Olympic trials. He was always a gentleman and became my best friend in track and field. While I was coaching at Chadron State College in Nebraska, Berny scheduled a trip from Oregon to New York City, to take a high jumper to Madison Square Garden. He found out that I had a track clinic going at that time, and he offered to come help.

"I'll just set down in Rapids City, South Dakota," he said.

So I drove up there, picked him up and he did a two-day clinic for me, free of charge. That's the kind of guy Berny has always been.

Recently, I asked if he could write a letter of encouragement to a high jumper who lives in a remote part of South Dakota. Berny penned a personal letter to him, offering pointers on the high jump.

If you add up his experiences in track and field—athlete, coach and administrator of ruling bodies—Berny is at the top. As a helpful personal friend, he has provided direction and information in many ways, to those of us involved in track and field.

* * * * *

Asked about his first experiences with sport, Wagner says, "During my childhood, I was always competitive. I picked berries off bushes and threw them at telephone poles or other targets during my mile walk/run to school—and I kept score of the hits. My first organized sports participation was in the 6th grade, when my dad took me to a kid's meet and I long-jumped 10'6".

"The crash (Depression) hit when we were in Redwood City, where Dad was manager of a branch of the Bank of Italy (which later became the Bank of America). My mother, sister and I were sent to live with my mom's folks for about six months. Dad became an employee of the California State Banking Administration, and we moved to Willows, California. Our financial situation was comfortable after that.

"In junior high, we had no formal coaching. I ran the 75-yard dash in the seventh grade, but didn't place. In the eighth grade, I tried the 150 yards and 330 yards, and still didn't place. In the ninth grade, however, I won the 660-yard run. That same year, I participated in the annual all-city swim meet and won ribbons in freestyle and the back stroke.

"In junior high, I was deeply involved in drama and musicals (I sang). I took piano lessons, but didn't practice much and therefore had little success. I stopped taking lessons when Class 'C' basketball practice started."

Wagner explains that in northern California, Class 'C' basketball was for young, short players, usually sophomores. "Players weighed in and received 'exponents' for each inch of height and each pound of weight, plus each month of age. If the total was less than a specific number, he could play on a class 'C' team. Between that number and a higher one, he could play 'B,' and so on to 'A,' which was varsity.

"Ability had nothing to do with where one was placed," he says, "just height, weight and age, combined. If an athlete was talented enough, he could 'move up,' but could not drop back a class during that season."

Wagner completed his sophomore and junior years at C.K. McClatchy High School, in Sacramento, California, where he competed in an inter-school cross-country meet in the fall of his sophomore year.

"The course was three quarters of a mile long," he says. "I hadn't trained for it, except for basketball practice. I lay down beside the track for a minute or two—got up, and placed 15th. Fifteen ribbons were awarded.

"By spring, I was classified as a 'B,' and competed in the 880 yards, for a very good 1940 'B' team. I set a McClatchy High School Class 'B' record in the 880 at 2:09.8.

"In 1940-41, I played center on the Class 'B' basketball team, and was named to the all-city team. I ran the 880 on the varsity team and had a personal best of 2:06.5. I also long-jumped, with a personal best of 19'10".

"Our family moved to Palo Alto during the summer between my junior and senior years. I was a second string player, behind the conference player of the year, on an undefeated team. Needless to say, I played very little. I ran varsity track as the number one half-miler, with a personal best of 2:04.8. My long jumping improved to 20'6".

"Academics were important to me. Neither of my parents were college graduates, but they emphasized getting good grades. I earned California Scholastic Federation ranking my senior year in high school. I hoped to eventually enter a field that had something to do with chemistry.

"War was declared in December 1941, and my mother died the next spring. I moved across the highway to Stanford University in the fall of 1942, played and lettered in freshman basketball and then went out for track as an 880 man.

"That season was a total disaster," Wagner says. "I spent more time in the training room with various injuries (some serious) than on the track. The one highlight of the '42 season was our freshman coach—Cornelius "Dutch" Warmerdam, who was doing his Master's degree work. He vaulted a lot during the spring and routinely cleared 15 feet in practice— before any other vaulter had cleared that height."

Warmerdam was the first man to clear 15 feet, and had 43 vaults over 15 feet before he was challenged. He held the world indoor record at 15 feet 8½ inches, and his 1942 outdoor vault of 15 feet 7¾ inches stood for 15 years. He was later head track coach at Fresno State.

"I joined the Navy V-12," Wagner says, "and was classified as a Specialist Engineer. I was an engineer in the Navy's eyes because I had started Stanford as a chemical engineering major. I was color-blind, but had not been aware of it until I took the Navy physical."

The V-12 program was established by the Navy in 1942 to help support the war effort, through accelerated officer training at American universities and colleges. Student enrollees were able to complete their studies, along with military training, before being commissioned in the Navy.

In July 1942, Wagner reported to Cal Tech in Pasadena, where he played basketball and made the varsity during the last part of the season. "Some of the teams we played had post-season stars," Wagner says, "including Olympians, and they usually beat us. We were, however, able to handle most of the college teams. For example, we split with USC and UCLA.

"In the spring, I was again an 880 man. I shaved one-tenth of a second off the Cal Tech record, taking it to 1:59.7. I ran the two mile relay, the 1320 leg on the distance medley and was scheduled for the mile as well."

By December of 1943, Wagner reports that he was disillusioned with engineering—more so because he'd been placed in mechanical engineering.

"I asked for, and received a transfer to boot camp," he says. "All of my high school friends were overseas by this time, and I wanted to be there, also. (Yes, we were crazy kids and wanted to get out and bite someone's jugular vein!)

"So the color-blind kid was put on a train for Great Lakes Naval Training Center in January of 1944, where I was put in a signal corps school. Whoops! They did a lot of signaling with colored wig-wag flags in those days.

"I was transferred to the Electricians Mate school," Wagner says, "which wasn't much better, since all wire was color coded. But after Cal Tech, electrician's mate school was a cinch, and I graduated in August of that year with the highest grade to that time, and received a 'Commendation Mast" (award for meritorious performance).

"I wanted to be a Specialist A (Athletic Specialist), but the candidates were many and the school was full. I was sent to an outgoing unit at San Francisco Treasure Island, for movement by troop transport to Guam. I was finally going to sea!

"However...," Wagner says, "the day we sailed under the Golden Gate Bridge turned out to be V-J Day (August 14, 1945—Victory over Japan). Bells were ringing, horns tooting; cannons at the Presidio were firing. We could even hear the yelling of the crowds.

"After ten months in the Pacific and Japan, the ship I was assigned to from Guam, the *John Q. Roberts, APD94*, sailed from Japan through the Panama Canal and was decommissioned in Green Cove Springs, Florida. I was shipped to California, with a *lot* of other guys, and was discharged in May.

"During the summer of 1945, I thought more and more about abandoning engineering and studying to be a coach," Wagner says. "During my college years, my favorite subjects were science, math and, of course, physical education. A great teacher, Tex Byrd, helped me figure out the right courses to take, and steered me toward a health minor.

"I re-entered Stanford that fall—in Education—and graduated in the spring of 1948. I had been married in December of 1946, and our daughter was born in October of 1947. I went on to complete a Masters degree in 1949.

"I ran for Stanford in the 1946 and 1947 seasons, with little success, clocking a best of 1:56.4 for 880 yards. I didn't letter either year. We did win the two mile relay at the Fresno Relays, beating USC for the watches.

"Then a strange thing happened," Wagner says. "My advisor called me in and told me I was ineligible my senior year because I had *too many* credits! Service credits had put me over the limit. Several athletes were set down from their sports because of this determination."

Wagner went on to be Clerk of the Course and assistant meet director for Jack Weiershouser, then the Stanford track coach. "I ran for the San Francisco Olympic Club, which was coached by Dink Templeton," he says, "but I was not impressive."

Before he coached the Olympic Club, Robert Lyman "Dink" Templeton coached Stanford track teams to three team and 19 individual titles in the NCAA. He was part of the U.S. gold medal rugby team at the 1920 Games in Antwerp, and placed fourth in the long jump.

"The next year was my first year of teaching and coaching," Wagner says, "and my retirement from competition came all at once. I had a job teaching six subjects and coaching all sports at a small high school [Wheatlands—population 500] in the Sacramento Valley. There were 80 students enrolled in the entire school. I was competing for the local Olympic Club, but found that there wasn't enough time for that." At Wheatland he coached all sports, drove the school bus, taught woodworking and family relations.

Wagner taught for 13 years in four California high schools. He taught 17 different physical education activities and coached five different sports. Wagner did not like to cut athletes from a sport, and was therefore more comfortable with individual, rather than team sports. Wagner developed and implemented a physical education curriculum of more than 20 activities for boys' and coed use. In the mid-fifties, when girls' competitive sports were rare, Wagner allowed a girls' track club to work out with his track team at San Mateo High School.

Wagner speaks candidly about a friendship that helped turn him to coaching in track and field. "This happened in Lodi, California," he says. "I started the 'C' basketball programs and the beginning of a cross-country program. We were playing another school in our gym, and my next-door neighbor was the referee.

"Something happened on the floor that I vehemently disagreed with, and I started an argument with my friend. He called a technical foul on me; I didn't stop. He called a second technical, but I kept ranting and raving, so he called a third technical. I finally quieted down.

"During the next few days, I realized that if I could lose control like that in a 'C' basketball game, track was a better sport for me. It wasn't long before my friend and I started talking to each other again, and even though I left Lodi the next year for a Bay area school, Ed and his wife, Joyce, have remained good friends, and we continue to visit each other."

When Wagner is asked about other people he keeps in touch with, he replies that he has many friends throughout the country. "I got to know people through my experiences at four high schools, the College of San Mateo, Stanford, Cal Tech, Oregon State University, and the PAC-8 Conference," he says. "I also gained colleagues from being executive director of TFA/USA (which represents all of the school and college organizations in the country), eight years as National Coach Coordinator for the Athletics Congress, (USATF—the national governing body for track and field), and being an assistant Olympic track coach.

"I enjoy visiting with these people at USATF annual conventions and track meets. Some have traveled all over the world, while others were neighbors in the 12 homes in the nine cities or towns that Nancy and I have lived in."

When asked about role models in sports, Wagner replies, "To me, a role model is someone who is fair, knows his field, is outgoing with the people he's associated with, and gives credit to others."

By all accounts, Berny Wagner meets his own criteria for the role model he has become for countless athletes and aspiring coaches.

Asked about retirement, Wagner says that he was involved in coaching track and field and in being an administrator for 39 years. "I retired from the Athletics Congress in 1989," he says (on his 65th birthday), "and moved to Salem, Oregon."

Since his retirement, Wagner has served on the Special Olympics International's National Athletic Staff for the Northwestern Region of the U.S., has taught in the Track Coaches Diploma Program, sponsored by the United States Track Coaches Association, and served as Technical Director for Athletics at the 1990 Goodwill Games. He was liaison to the U.S. Olympic Committee for Development and the Elite Athlete Programs. Wagner also initiated and implemented the Athletics Congress drug testing and control program.

Wagner was a featured lecturer on the preparation of coaches for the Mexican government in 1963; at the International Track and Field Coaches Association Congress in Spain in 1973, and in India in 1977.

"I was out of the sport for three months when I was asked to assist at Western Oregon College [now Western Oregon University] with the high jumpers. I thought it would be a nice activity for a year or two. Now, 14 years later, I have added to my 39 years in the sport and made it 53!" he says.

"During my time at Western, I've helped athletes in the high jump win 16 NAIA titles (National Association of Intercollegiate Athletics), Division II All American honors (nine women and six men), including three NAIA championships. In the 2003-2004 school year, I plan to occasionally consult with the next high jump coach and his athletes."

Asked to comment on the topic of amateurism, Wagner says that he believes that separating "amateur" and "professional" in track and field is a good idea. "Even though collegiate athletes receive money for education (although many don't, he says), in our system they are amateurs, as are high school and local club athletes. The fact is," Wagner adds, "many club athletes pay for the privilege of competing for their club.

"The very top athlete can 'go pro,'" Wagner says. "In any society which gets above a subsistence level, there is a move toward sport. *Homo sapiens* are competitive. The Olympics should have the best athletes in the world competing in them. We need to rethink the whole idea of what amateurism means.

"In the U.S., we have the best system in the world, through our schools and colleges, for amateur competition. As we continue to develop more and more elite athletes in each sport, we have a better chance than any other place in the world to continue competition for sub-elite athletes who want to participate."

Asked about the drug problem in sports, Wagner replies, "I think the obvious regulatory bodies are going in the right direction in trying to stop performance-enhancing drug use. Whether they will achieve 100 percent success is doubtful," he adds.

When asked what sports have meant to him, Wagner says "The things that mean the most to me are not documented. They are comments or letters from former high school and college athletes. An excerpt from a former student illustrates the positive influence Wagner had on his athlete's lives:

> Dear Coach,
>   This letter is so long overdue that I am almost ashamed to write it. However, my mother once said that it is never too late to acknowledge a kindness. I want to take this opportunity to let you know that I think of you constantly with gratitude and appreciation for the many things you taught me and the opportunities you provided.
>   Without your intervention, I may not have gone to college; I would not have found the job at the *Redwood City Tribune*, which supported my wife and me until we completed graduate school.
>   Finally, I would not have realized that all around you are people who care about your well-being and positive life outcomes.
>   Coach Wagner, it was always obvious that you cared about everyone. You did so without regard for their status on the team, the team they were on, or any other distinctions that people use to set each of us apart, one from the other. You molded men of strength and conviction—free of arrogance, confident of their skills and aware of their limitations.
>   In reflecting back over the last forty years, the bright moments at San Mateo High are always part of my life's highlight film. I remember you examining the report cards, not for eligibility, but rather to challenge those in need of such, to put forth greater effort. I was one such student. I don't believe I would have succeeded to the extent that I have without that challenge.
>
>   Sam Rutland

"I haven't made much money," Wagner concludes, "but it's been a great life."

17

Archie Franklin Williams

LONG SPRINTS • GOLD MEDAL 400 METERS
Born May 1, 1915, Oakland, California
Died June 24, 1993, Fairfax, California

In 1935, Archie Williams transferred from San Mateo Junior College to the University of California to study mechanical engineering. Under the direction of legendary coach, Brutus Hamilton, Williams developed his track skills and set a world record of 46.1 in the 400-meter race, in the preliminary heats for the NCAA finals. He placed first in the finals with a 47.0, and went on to win the gold medal in the 400 meters at the 1936 Berlin Games, with a 46.5. It was a magnificent year and full of promise for future triumphs on the field.

Unfortunately, Williams' running career came to a premature end, with a serious leg injury just a year later. Williams became a pilot and flying instructor. During World War II, he served in the U.S. Army Air Corps and taught the famed Tuskegee Airmen. After the war, he continued his military career for 20 more years, serving as a flight instructor and weather officer. Williams retired in 1965 with the rank of Lieutenant Colonel. Following his retirement from the military, Williams taught math and computing at high schools in Marin County, California, from 1965 until 1987, when he retired at the age of 72.

Career Achievements

- As a freshman at San Mateo Junior College, Williams won the conference championship in the 400 meters.
- In his sophomore year, Williams anchored a relay team for the University of California that competed as an unknown in the

Archie Williams (long sprints). (Courtesy Archie Williams.)

Long Beach Relays, and staged an upset victory over teams from Stanford and the University of Southern California.

• In 1936, Williams won the Pacific Coast Conference 400 meters with a 46:8, and the NCAA Championship with a 47.0.

• Williams is tied for seventh place on the all-time list for the 400 meters at the University of California.

• Williams was in the first class of distinguished graduates inducted into the University of California Athletic Hall of Fame, established in 1986.

• He was inducted into the Track and Field Hall of Fame in 1992.

• The Archie Williams Drake Alumni Scholarship is awarded yearly to a student from Drake High School, where Williams taught for 22 years.

Interview

"I was told not to aim too high because I was going to fail. My idea is to aim twice as high as you think you can go—then maybe you will get there."

Interviewer's Notes

I interviewed Archie Williams just across the street from the Jesse Owens Track at Ohio University, during the reunion of the 1936 Olympians. When I first met Archie, I was impressed with his still youthful appearance and enthusiasm. As we talked, it was apparent that Archie was a person who set goals and stuck by them. He discussed at length his second career as a high school teacher, focusing on the need to give young people direction.

* * * * *

"I grew up in the East Bay area of San Francisco," Williams says. "I was a local boy who grew up in the shadow of the Campanile, which is the big tower at the University of California. [Sather Tower, known as the Campanile, is a long-standing symbol of the University of California at Berkeley. Built in 1914, it stands 307 feet tall.] One of my earliest ambitions was to somehow get to go to that school and ultimately do some sports there. It certainly wasn't something I thought up overnight; it had been my dream since I was a little kid."

Williams was named for his grandfather, Army Sergeant, Archy Wall, who served in the Spanish American War. He was stationed at the Presidio in San Francisco, and after his time in service, the family settled in Oakland. Williams' middle name "Franklin" comes from his mother's family; Aretha Franklin is a distant relative. His father came from Chicago. He owned a grocery store and sold real estate, but died of pneumonia when Williams was ten years old.

"It was in elementary school that I first became interested in sports. They had the 50-yard dash and the standing long jump. I did pretty well in some events, but I had no illusions to do much past that, except I could beat most of the girls and a few of the boys."

"When I got to high school, all my friends were going out for track so I went along with them. I won a few easy races, but in the big competition I was usually back in the pack."

Williams played basketball, volleyball and sandlot baseball when he was growing up. He and his friends sometimes staged track meets, with a 50-yard dash and the long jump.

"My friends and I finished high school," he says, "and I just kicked around for awhile. We were in the Depression and there were no jobs. I found just enough odd jobs, caddying and that sort of work, to keep things together. My buddy said we should go back to school. He thought we should go to the junior college down at San Mateo. It wouldn't cost us much and we could learn something.

"I asked him what he wanted to do and he said, 'I think I will be a dentist.' My choice was to be an engineer and I told him I was going to take a crack at that. We both went to San Mateo. It was necessary for both of us to make up credits because high school hadn't been that attractive to us. We would need those credits to get into a big school.

"We went to school for a year or so, and it was there I got to work under a good coach by the name of Tex Bird. Tex did not con anybody about their ability, but he told me I had some promise, if I wanted to go for it. I had been running the 100 and 200 meters and Tex suggested I try the quarter mile. 'It's a tough road,' he said, 'but once you have it down, it will be an event that you can show promise in.'

"It was my second semester in school and Coach got me going. I was knocking seconds off my time and by the end of the season, I was running under 50 seconds. Now I was ready to go to the big school! I went over to the University of California at Berkeley and enrolled.

"I don't think anyone knew I was there until fall track practice started.

I worked out and didn't do anything spectacular, although I was getting better. When spring season rolled around, track season started and Brutus Hamilton was my coach.

"He told me the same thing Tex said, 'You can go as far as you want to.'

"I took Coach Hamilton for his word and started working hard. Brutus was, first of all, a great human being and that is what he projected. (Incidentally, **Glenn Cunningham** also had a lot to do with whatever success I had.) Brutus was interested in each of us as individuals—a person and a student. He knew every grade we were making in every class and every test.

"He wouldn't make a big thing about it, but he knew just where you stood at all times. 'Don't neglect your classes,' he said, 'that's what you're here for.' Anyone would have been proud to have Brutus for a coach or a friend. He never lost sight of the fact that you were a human being. Your life and what you did was more important than anything on the track."

The versatile Hamilton, already a legend for his coaching at the University of Kansas, was an English major in college, won a tryout for the New York Yankees, and was a boxing champion in the Army.

Williams competed in the 1936 Olympics in Berlin. Because Adolf Hitler had frequently stated his belief in the inferiority of blacks, there was some concern at the University about Williams participating in the Berlin Olympics. The Men's Athletic Council believed it would be more positive for Williams and other black athletes to attend, and prove Hitler wrong. They unanimously approved endorsement of their athletes for the 1936 Olympics, where nine black athletes, including Archie Williams (University of California), **John Woodruff** (University of Pittsburgh) and Jesse Owens (Ohio State), won more medals than the rest of the U.S. track and field team, combined (8 gold, 3 silver, and 1 bronze).

Archie Williams won the 400-meter gold; James LuValle won the bronze in that race; John Woodruff place first in the 800; Jesse Owens won the 100, 200 and long jump gold medals; Ralph Metcalfe took the silver in the 100-meter race, and Mac Robinson placed second behind Owens in the 200. The winning 4 × 100 relay included both Owens and Metcalfe; Cornelius Johnson won first place in the high jump, followed by David Albritton in second.

Athletes were given Olympic oaks to plant on their respective campuses. Williams tried to send his back home, but customs would not allow the oak tree into the country.

When the conversation moves to William's memories of the 1936 Olympics, he says, "There were not many participants in the 400 meters.

The first day we had the prelims at 10 o'clock in the morning. At 2 P.M., we ran the second set of preliminaries. The next day at 3:30 in the afternoon, we ran the semi-finals, and an hour and a half later we had the finals. They packed it together pretty tightly and it was almost a matter of survival. It was tough," Williams says, "but it was tough on all of us.

"Coach Hamilton always told us: 'Look, some of these guys want to save themselves in a race. Every race that you run is a final. If you don't win, then it *is* final.'"

Of the day itself, Williams says: "For me to try and remember the race is as difficult as trying to remember the day I was born. There were so many people in the stands—so much noise and excitement—it actually ended up being somewhat of a humbling experience. I really didn't feel anything except the thought that here is a race I have to run. I wasn't kidding myself about how important it was, but at the same time, I told myself to just do what I was supposed to do and see how it comes out.

"I do remember that we had to draw the lane numbers out of a hat. I usually got the outside lane, but this time I was lucky and drew the next to the outside lane. When you run the outside lanes it means you can't see the other guys until you come around for the finish.

"My biggest concern, which seems silly now," Williams says, "was that when we came around the final turn and the lanes all merged together like the train tracks in a railroad yard, I was definitely afraid I might step out of my lane on that turn.

"Well it turned out that I didn't. It was such a relief; I guess it allowed me to put together whatever else I had to finish the race. The biggest concern I had then was whether I could make it around that turn without fouling.

"After the race was over and they told me I had won, I felt really good—it was a very close race, and it took me a couple days to appreciate what had happened. In fact, over 50 years later, I am wondering if it really happened.

"During the time I was competing, there was still a lot of racial tension. There were places, even in California, where you couldn't eat. I couldn't join the Boy Scouts. When I went to the meeting this guy says, 'We aren't ready for you yet.' I couldn't swim in the YMCA pool. All this didn't bother me too much, as some of my family had grown up in the South and I was aware of these kinds of things.

"At Cal, I signed up for mechanical engineering and the counselor said, 'Are you sure you want to take that?'

"I replied, 'Sure I do.'

"He went on to suggest I go into real estate or become a lawyer. He told me I wouldn't get a job in engineering, but I told him to sign me up and I would worry about that when the time came.

"In many ways that counselor was right, because when I graduated in '39, there weren't any jobs. I ended up learning how to fly a plane. I received my pilot's license and went down to Tuskegee, Alabama, as a flying instructor."

Williams was a lifelong airplane enthusiast; as a youngster, he won a prize in the *Oakland Tribune* model airplane contest.

"My parents were supportive of anything I wanted to do," Williams says. "No one in my family up to that time had ever been to college. They didn't push me into going. I told my mother I wanted to go to college and my family said they would help me as much as they could. My father died when I was ten, and my mother worked. We were still in the Depression and everyone pitched in. The attitude was that if you want to do it, do it," he says. "With respect to my going to college, I would have to say that I was very well supported. I felt as though I had a mission to accomplish."

Williams had an admirable, supportive family. His grandmother, Fannie Wall, founded the Fannie Wall Children's Home in Oakland, a child care center and orphanage. Mrs. Wall was good friends with Mary McCloud Bethune (renowned African-American educator and activist), who stayed with the Williams family during a conference in 1929.

Williams said, "During the time I was competing in high school, we didn't have fancy uniforms and it depended on who marked the track whether it was 440 yards or 430 yards. Sometimes there was sawdust in the high jump pit and sometimes there wasn't. It was a little bit above playground activity level.

"It wasn't a question of discipline, it was a matter that everyone got a suit, spikes, and that all of us pitched in fixing hurdles or dragging the track. It was a lot of fun and it was organized, but not over-organized. You had the feeling you were doing about what you did on the playgrounds during the summer.

"It was fun to compete against other schools, but there wasn't a lot of hoopla. Most of the coaches in those days were your physical education teachers. It seems the trend now is to recruit coaches from the community. It is difficult to get people from within the school to work for what they pay them. Sometimes coaching is an invitation to disaster.

"I'm not much of a philosopher, but it seems to me that kids nowadays have a buzz word and that is 'boredom.' It's difficult to say what causes it. Maybe it has to do with all the media. It's so easy for a young person to experience so much. In effect, what else is new?

"I've seen some students turn to sports to escape from what they experience as boredom. It's not that they want to be a jock, but they're looking for something different. Others turn to religion. They want to try out everything.

"There will always be a certain number of kids who are into sports," Williams says. "It's an opportunity to excel—show what they can do and be recognized. More and more we have gone to participatory sports, especially for the girls and for younger and smaller kids."

Williams retired from teaching in 1987, at the age of 72. "My concern in the broader sense," he says, "is the attitude children have about what they are going to do with their lives. Many of our schools seem to be teenage daycare centers. It's the easy way out for teachers to say, 'Here's the material and what you have to do. Turn it in at the end of the period, and at the end of the week you will have a quiz.' There is no personal contact; no one-on-one. Yet the teacher says, 'I did my share, I taught them.'

"This same story has its parallel in many coaching situations. Young teachers and coaches are the innovators and that is what I am really worried about. The system tends to squelch innovation, initiative and creativity for the sake of uniformity and homogeneity. The result is a nice crop of mediocre kids. The message is: 'Don't challenge them.'

"Many of my students are impressed with my being an Olympic champion. The first question they ask me is, 'Did you run with Jesse Owens?'"

Williams laughs: "I tell them, 'Jesse James, too.'

"They tell me about being in the library and seeing my picture. Some students have told me that their fathers read about me and that they would like to meet me some day. Every four years, during the Olympic year, the social studies teachers want me to talk about the world situation—Hitler and that stuff.

"I don't like being pessimistic, but many things are going to have to change, to get the Olympics back where they belong. I fear greatly that the Olympics have become such a spectacle, that some of the original objectives have been lost.

"For example, in preparation for one of the Olympics, there was a little girl who was an ice skater. She was asked during an interview about some of the things she had to do in preparation for the games. One question was, 'What was one of the most important things your coach told you to do?'

"She replied, 'Get a nose job, because you will get more points if you look prettier.'

"The old Olympic motto was 'Higher, Faster, Further.' Now they might as well put in 'prettier.' In this day and age, you can also add 'richer.'

The main objective of the Games should be for a bunch of young people to get together for a celebration. They should compete, and when it's all over, shake hands and agree to do it again in four years.

"Presently, the Olympics are so commercial. They stop events to advertise the athletes and the companies they represent. The Games have grown so darn big, that they are unwieldy. Let's face it—the world is twice as big as it was fifty years ago. This means there are twice as many athletes—twice as many *good* athletes.

"In the '36 games, it took a week to run it off; now it takes almost three weeks. There are many events that weren't even around then. The more events you add, the more it dilutes the thing, with respect to the original games.

"One solution might be to have the athletics portion of the Olympics outdoors. These sports would represent the summer Olympics. The aquatics would make up the next Olympics. I believe this would be as large as the outdoor Olympics. The winter Olympics are already established. The final Olympics would be made up of indoor sports such as wrestling, boxing, and basketball.

"The opening ceremony takes all day and, of course, the saddest part is the nationalism involved. In 1936 this really got started. It was a very political affair and, as a result, detailed scores were kept, or at least they tried to keep score. Every country, of course, had its own system. Whatever gave you the most points was the way to keep score.

"Athletics has given me a lot of confidence in myself," Williams says. "It made me realize that if I tried hard, there was a chance to succeed. You may not get exactly what you want, but you can succeed in life, and that is something that is going to help everyone.

"When I was a pilot, I knew I could handle situations. Even if I had not won the Olympics, I still would have felt good about myself. I ate enough dust, too, not to become cocky. In fact, there was one good runner to whom I said, 'Let me look at your face. Wow! This is the first time I have ever seen your face. I always had a view of your butt and the back of your head.' He was one of my high school competitors and is now a judge in San Francisco.

"I believe that any athlete who starts out being a success from day one is missing out on something. You have to get a little bitterness in there and you gotta be hungry. I have seen kids who were highly successful up to the time they really got into some competition and they couldn't handle the idea that there was somebody who could beat them. I ate a lot of humble pie and stayed in there for the big meal.

"I coached track in Marin County. We had a county meet and my runner came in eighth and was crying. I said, 'You feel pretty bad, don't you?' I went on and said, 'Do you know how many 15-year-old kids there are in this county? Well, there are about 7,000 and how many of them can beat you?'

"I sometimes get asked what it felt like to be the fastest man in the world. My answer is, 'What the hell are you talking about? I just happened to be the fastest guy that showed up that day.' You go to Africa and you will find some guy down there that breaks my record every day just running for a meal or from being a meal! So, don't talk about being the fastest in the world, because the world is a big place and you haven't checked it all out.

"A year after the Olympics I had some bad luck with leg injuries. I was taking engineering in college, which was tough enough by itself, so I couldn't see myself putting out a lot of extra time for maybe another successful year. I said, 'Well, I had a crack at it and a chance to go all the way, so why not get on with something else?'

"Studying engineering was a big challenge," he says. "I always remembered the counselor telling me I wasn't going to make it. I was told not to aim too high because I was going to fail. My idea is to aim twice as high as you think you can go, then maybe you will get there. I felt that somewhere along the line, I had to pass this on.

"Distance runners these days don't reach their peak until their late 20s. We went out and ran for fun. I couldn't work out seven days a week, twice a day. I don't believe it would mean that much to me just to whack off a little of my time. My friends and I saw running as a nice activity that was good and challenging. Everyone was in the same boat; we didn't kill ourselves with workouts.

"These guys now are in a grim business. You go to a track meet now, and nobody is smiling. They frown and growl and try to psyche someone out. That isn't what it is all about. Some might ask 'If you don't want to win, why bother?' but I'd say, 'Sure I want to win, but not at all costs.' I want to win by just doing the best I can, and letting the chips fall where they may. I don't want to psyche someone out or take a pill that will give me the edge. I guess it is just a different world and maybe it has sort of passed some of us by. I was happy with the way it was.

"The Olympics, as originally conceived, are not there anymore—as a celebration and a get-together for the athletes. There are things like the World Games, and I kind of like that. But there is a mystique about the circles on the Olympic flag. The idea is worth saving, but when you have to save it by throwing money at it and not putting your heart into it, then that is bad."

18

John Woodruff

MIDDLE DISTANCES • GOLD MEDAL
800 METER
Born July 5, 1915, Connellsville, Pennsylvania

Just after finishing his freshman year at the University of Pittsburgh, John Woodruff qualified for the Olympic Games in the 800-meter race. In Berlin, he was slow at the start, and was soon boxed in by more experienced runners.

With a strategy that New York *Herald-Tribune* sports writer Jesse Abramson called "the most daring move seen on a track," Woodruff slowed to a stop, let the pack run past him, and began the race again, this time taking the outside lane.

Running the longest race of all his competitors, he out-distanced them and won the gold, with a time of 1:52.9. Sports writers since that time have wondered what Woodruff's time would have been if he'd had a fast start in the race.

Woodruff graduated from the University of Pittsburgh in 1939 with a bachelor's degree in sociology. In 1941, he completed work on a master's degree in sociology from New York University. After a career in the military, Woodruff taught school in New York City and worked with the New York City Children's Aid Society. He was a parole officer for the State of New York, Recreation Center Director for the New York City Police Athletic League, and a special investigator for the New York Department of Welfare.

John Woodruff (middle distances) hitting the finish line in 1936. (Courtesy John Woodruff.)

Career Achievements

- In his first track competition in high school, Woodruff won both the 880 and the mile runs.

- He broke existing school records in middle distances at the school, county and state levels.

- In 1935, Woodruff set a new national high school mile record with a 4:23.4.

- Woodruff won three back-to-back NCAA titles in the 800 meters and three IC4A championships in the 440- and 880-yard runs.

- He won the National AAU title in 1937 for the 880-yard run.

- In 1940, he set a new U.S. record in the 800 meters, and was a member of the national 4 × 880-yard team that won the world title. He also ran a record-breaking half-mile run at the Cotton Bowl in Dallas.

- Woodruff was inducted into the Track and Field Hall of Fame in 1978.

Interview

"Actually, I started the race twice. I was told that no time in the history of running had a race been run that way!"

Interviewer's Notes

John Woodruff was one of America's youngest athletes in the 1936 Berlin Olympic Games. As a 19-year-old University of Pittsburgh freshman, representing the U.S. in the 800 meters, John ran, as he says, "a strange and complicated race," that amazed spectators and won him the gold medal. World War II cut short Woodruff's opportunity to participate in another Olympic competition, but coaches believe that he could have been the first sub-four-minute miler.

Each gold medal Olympian at the Berlin Games was presented with an oak sapling. Woodruff presented his oak to the city of Connellsville, and it was planted at the south end of the city football stadium. Visitors regularly gather acorns from the ground, as historic mementos. Twenty-four of these oaks are still growing around the world. Of the five U.S. sites searched for acorns, the Woodruff tree was the only one producing seeds.

I had carried on correspondence with Woodruff about the Olympic Oaks when he was in California and later when he was in New Jersey. When I went to Connellsville, I stopped by the *Courier* newspaper, and it was evident from talking to people that John was very well liked and respected. He had been welcomed home with a parade atteded by an estimated 10,000 people.

Woodruff was given the nick-name "Black Shadow of Pittsburgh" by the renowned sportswriter and author, Damon Runyon. He was also dubbed "Long John" Woodruff by sports writers, because of his nine foot stride. James M. Driscoll, publisher of the *Connellsville Courier*, called him "Seven League Boots," a reference to the fairy tale "Puss in Boots," where magical boots enabled their wearer to take seven leagues in a single stride (a league is about 3 miles).

* * * * *

"Track has been one of the big things in my life," Woodruff said, as he began the interview, "but I didn't participate until I was a junior in high school at Connellsville. I did reasonably well my first year of running, but I really came into my own during my senior year by setting a new state record in the mile—4:23.4. My half-mile at that time (1935) was 1:55.1 and my quarter mile, 48.3.

"Times were rather hard back in those days. If I hadn't received a scholarship, I could never have gone to college. On my first day at the University of Pittsburgh our sheriff transported me there. The only money I had in my pocket was 25 cents—that's all I had to my name. I had to find the coach and get some money for food. He gave me $5, and that money lasted me a whole week."

When Woodruff went to Pittsburgh as a student, he roomed at the YMCA. By eating 5-cent hamburgers and 20-cent hot beef sandwiches, Woodruff made the $5 the track coach gave him for food last a week. Woodruff earned room and board his first year by working with the cleaning crew for the football stadium and basketball gym. A job as a groundsman for the university finally allowed him to eat in the cafeteria.

"I came from a poor family," Woodruff says. "My mother had died in 1934, and my father was a laborer. He dug coal, carried hod (cement for laying bricks) and worked in the steel mills. He was a very powerful man.

"I came out of a large family. There were 12 of us, and I was next to the youngest. Many died in infancy, from diseases such as measles, whooping cough, pneumonia and scarlet fever.

"I was always a quite fast runner," Woodruff remembers, "but I never realized that I was going to develop into a championship runner. I never had any dreams that something like that was going to happen. In football we used to run wind sprints up and down the field. The quarterback was the star sprinter, and the line coach [Joseph "Pop" Larew] noticed I was able to keep up with him. He then invited me out for track.

"I quit football one week before our first game," Woodruff says. "I was forced to quit because my mother told me I was getting home too late, and there were chores to do. But when I was out for track, I could get home at a reasonable time.

"I never realized I had that speed, until it was pointed out to me. The coach told me that if I worked hard I would have a chance to go to college. I dropped everything and started to concentrate on track.

"I used to go to the mountains and pick blackberries and other fruit from abandoned farms. I would bring the fruit home and whatever my mother didn't can, I would sell. From those sales, I picked up a little extra spending money. I picked up junk to sell and gathered greens. I also had a job in the brickyard cleaning the concrete off the bricks.

"The black community in Connellsville, Pennsylvania, where I come from consisted of two black families in my neighborhood. So, I was always with white people. All my playmates were white. In fact, I never had a fight with anyone of my race in my life. When I got to the University of Pittsburgh there were only three blacks on the track team.

"As a high school kid, I was really interested in going to Ohio State. I'd met Jesse Owens and had heard so much about him, that I wanted to be with somebody like him. But the business people in my hometown were good alums, and of course they encouraged me to go to Pittsburgh.

"When I went to Pitt my freshman year [1935], I participated in the Allegheny Association Meet, where I ran the 440 and the half mile. That qualification enabled me to run in the Olympic semi-finals at Harvard Stadium. I went up there and ran the half-mile against Charlie Hornbostel from Indiana, and several other half milers." Hornbostel ran sixth in the 800 meters in the 1932 Olympics. and fifth in 1936.

"I won the race and that qualified me for the finals, which were held at Randall's Island in New York. There, I faced Ben Eastman, one of the great half milers from California (Stanford), and defeated him. In fact, he didn't make the team. He was tough and a very fine quarter-miler too." Eastman, considered one of the finest quarter-mile and half-mile runners of his time, won the silver in the 400 meters at the 1932 Olympics. He held world outdoor records in the 400 meters, 440 yards, 500 meters, 600 yards, 800 meters and 880 yards.

Woodruff adds that the four coaches for the Olympic team included

Lawson Robertson, Dean Cromwell, Brutus Hamilton, and Billy Hayes. Cromwell, Hamilton and Hayes were inducted into the Track and Field Hall of Fame. Robertson won the bronze in the standing high jump in 1904, the silver in 1906; and the bronze in the standing long jump in 1906. In 1909, he set a world record of 11.0 for the three-legged 100-yard race with Harry Hillman that still stands.

The legendary Dean Cromwell, known as the "Maker of Champions," was coach at the University of Southern California for 39 years. He coached ten Olympic gold medal winners and 36 U.S. Olympic team members.

Brutus Hamilton, coach at the University of California in Berkeley, was an Olympic decathlete and pentathlete. His athletes broke two world records, seven national collegiate records and seven Olympic records, and included middle distance runner Don Bowden, the first American to break the 4 minute mile.

Billy Hayes coached at Indiana University from 1925 to 1943, and mentored some of the finest distance runners of the time, including three members of the National Track and Field Hall of Fame.

Woodruff says, "Even before the race, the coaches said very little. We were on our own. I was so naïve that I never knew what was in front of me. Everything happened so fast. If I would have known, I would probably have done more work. I did have that competitive spirit, though, and I guess I was born with it. In playground sports as a little kid, I always tried to excel.

"The only time I was really up against it was in the finals at the Olympics," Woodruff says. "Mac Robinson [Jackie Robinson's older brother], a teammate of mine, told me that I ran a 'dumb' race. I told him that you run a 'dumb' race if you lose.

"When I ran the preliminaries, which was the first race, I got a lead and kept it. When I ran in the semi-finals I did the same thing. [Woodruff outran international favorites, Kazamiere of Poland and Carlos Anderson of Argentina by twenty yards.]

"But I decided on my own that I would not take the lead in the final race. I was going to conserve myself for that final kick. I let Phil Edwards [Canada—five bronze medals in three Olympic Games] take the lead, but this was his program, too, and as a result, he set a very slow pace. He was going to conserve his strength for the kick.

"Now I was in trouble," Woodruff says. "What I should have done, when he set that slow pace, was just go out in front. But I stayed in the back of the field for the first quarter and when we finished that first lap going into the first turn I couldn't get out.

"I was in a perfect box, and the only way I could get out was to practically stop. I did this in the third lane, and started to run around the field. With my long stride there was no way for me to cut through, no way in the world without fouling somebody. So I went around them, because I had enough time, about 300 meters from the finish. The phenomenal thing was that I was able to break that rhythm and still pick it up again.

"Actually, I started the race twice. I was told that no time in the history of running had a race been run that way! When I went around the field from the third lane and had passed everybody in the field, Phil passed me again, and finally I passed him. The man who was favored to win that race from Italy [Mario Lanzi] was never ahead. I always ran out front after that." It was the first time in 24 years that the U.S. team brought home the gold in the 800-meter race.

Jim Worrel, Phil Edward's teammate and a student at McGill University with Edwards, describes how the race looked from the spectator's point of view:

> Woodruff was a huge man and he had a tremendous stride. It was interesting that he passed Phil, and then Phil passed him. And then down the backstretch on the second lap, it was rather amusing to watch, because all of a sudden these two bodies started to merge, and you could see one body but four legs [From "Phil Edwards: The Man of Bronze," an interview for CBC Sports Online. *The Olympians: A Century of Canadian Heroes*].

"If I would have jumped out in front," Woodruff speculates, "that race would have probably gone in 1:47+. My best time ever was 1:47.6. The next year at the Texas Centennial I ran 1:47.8 for a world's record.

"I had the speed and was capable of running a good quarter mile," Woodruff says. "To be a good half miler you also had to be a good 440 man, and I ran consistent 47 second quarters. In the IC4A I won the 440 and 700 doubles, three years in succession. In the last race, I was clocked in the quarter at 45.9, but they didn't give it to me. The world's record at the time was 46.4."

When Woodruff is asked about the influence of sports in his life, he says: "Sports made it possible for me to go to college. It was the biggest plus in my life, because I never could have attended, otherwise. No member of my immediate family ever went to college. My high school coach told me I could go to college and how much it would mean for me and my family.

"I was always the kind of kid, that if adults told me anything, I would listen and respond. I considered my coach like my father; he treated me like a father would.

"As far as the drug situation in sports goes," Woodruff says, "I really don't know what we can do about it. It's a terrible situation, and I am so glad that we came along when we did. What I don't understand with regard to drugs, is why athletes get involved with them in the first place. When I was engaged in sports I had a tremendous concern about my physical as well as my mental well-being. I wouldn't have dreamed of doing something that was detrimental to me.

"Some athletes are taking steroids to build muscle and give them strength. They know there are going to be some after-effects—a price to pay. But they don't seem to care. They are only interested in getting that medal. I believe that commercial interests are causing athletes to use drugs—to become millionaires. Amateurism is gone.

"I majored in sociology at Pitt, and received my masters from the school of education at New York University. My job was social investigator for the City of New York, and heading up a youth center for disadvantaged kids in Harlem. From there I worked as state parole officer for the State of New York.

"My final work was with the Job Corps. It was important to the kids I worked with that I had done well in athletics. They looked up to me and I became a role model for them. Look what **Glenn Cunningham** did over the years to help kids out. And that's just a drop in the bucket."

Woodruff believes that the lack of role models is hurting a lot of young athletes today. "All kids pick someone and want to be like them," he says. "If an athlete takes dope, young kids believe they can do that too. This all makes for a very poor role model. The situation is so broad, so vast—it is universal. Here in the U.S. we may have the bulk of it, since we are the richest nation in the world and have the money to buy the stuff.

"When we went to the '36 Olympic reunion in 1986, we realized that a few years make a lot of difference. We didn't talk about age, however. We talked about things we did in the past—jokes that we pulled during our early athletic days.

"We are often asked about Hitler and the '36 Olympics. When we got to Germany we were not interested in politics. We just wanted to do the best job that we could do. We did have some interest in what Hitler was doing. Many of us had read *Mien Kampf* and thought he was crazy. The plans he outlined in that book were what followed, but nobody believed him at the time.

"At the 1936 Olympics, the gold medalists were each given a small potted oak tree. When the trees were brought into the U.S., they had to go to Washington, where they checked the dirt in the pots for disease.

When I got back with mine, it was practically dead. I took it to my botany teacher and he worked with the tree. They planted it on the Carnegie Library lawn in Connellsville, Pennsylvania.

"When they built the Connellsville Stadium, which they were going to name after me, they moved the tree from the library up to the stadium. That tree is now about 50 feet high and very healthy. For many years there was nothing there to indicate what the tree was.

"When I was home, I had a talk with some of the people at the *Connellsville Courier* newspaper and asked them why there wasn't something up there to identify the tree, so that the kids could learn what it was all about. At that time, it was just another tree. The *Pittsburgh* and *Connellsville Courier* got together and built an identifying plaque.

"My friend Cornelius Johnson, a gold medal high jumper, planted his tree in his yard in Los Angeles," Woodruff says. It is commonly thought that Jesse Owens was the black athlete snubbed by Hitler at the 1936 Olympics. But it was Johnson's award ceremony that Hitler left before the medals were presented.

"Many of our great high school athletes did not go to college. I was lucky to be able to take advantage of the opportunity. Other athletes from around the country never had the opportunity to reach their full potential. Eulace Peacock [Columbia University] didn't make the '36 Olympic team. If he had, Jesse Owens might not have won the four gold medals. Peacock beat Owens seven out of the last ten times they ran.

"Ralph Metcalfe would have beaten him, if he'd gotten off the same time as Jesse in the 100 meters. [Metcalfe held 11 AAU titles and was a four time Olympic medalist—later a U.S. senator.] The week following the Berlin Games, he beat him, in Cologne, Germany. Metcalfe was a silver medalist in the 1932 Games, and at 27 years old, was not in his prime as a sprinter."

After the 1936 Games, Woodruff accompanied fellow Olympians on a tour of Europe, competing in local meets in Dresden, Oslo, London and Paris.

"Eulace Peacock and Ben Johnson from Columbia University both pulled muscles that same year," Woodruff adds. Peacock rivaled Jesse Owens for speed and versatility. He was the AAU pentathlon champion six times and held the world record in the 100-meter dash, defeating both Owens and Metcalfe, with a time of 10.2. Johnson was a national collegiate champion who went on to hold indoor records in the 200-yard dash, the 100-meter dash, and the 55-meter dash.

Woodruff pauses to savor the idea of his dream team. "If those two men would have made the team ... think about the relay they could have run," he says, finally: "Ben Johnson, Eulace Peacock, Ralph Metcalfe and Jesse Owens!"

Woodruff entered the service in 1941 as a 2nd Lieutenant, and was discharged at the end of World War II in 1945 with the rank of Captain. He re-entered the service during the Korean War and retired from the Army as a Lieutenant Colonel in 1957. During his time of service, Woodruff commanded two battalions, and was an executive officer for five different artillery battalions.

Every summer, the John Woodruff 5K Run and Walk is held in Connellsville. Woodruff returns to be the official starter and trophies presenter. He gave his athletic medals and Olympic sweater to Connellsville High School in 1976.

Don Holst of McKendree College in Lebanon, Illinois, grew saplings from acorns from Woodruff's oak, hoping to plant the trees in locations symbolic for track and field. On November 17, 1987, the first sapling was presented to the National Track and Field Hall of Fame and to the Athletics Congress/USA. It was planted near the National Track and Field Hall of Fame Historical Research Library (then Butler University in Indianapolis, Indiana).

The Library has since moved to the American Athletic Federation headquarters in California. In the library holdings, there is a folder which contains the historical background material about the original trees; an interview with John Woodruff; newspaper clippings; and an audio cassette tape of the planting ceremony.

Of the 50 seedlings raised from acorns by Don Holst, one became the International Honor Tree for National Arbor Day Foundation.

Appendix A:
Athletes and Coaches
Listed by Date of Birth

The athletes in this book touch three centuries. Two were born in the 19th century; all competed in the 20th century. Thirteen are still alive in the 21st.

Abel Kiviat—middle distances b. June 23, 1892
Jackson Scholz—sprints b. March 15, 1897
Ken Doherty—decathlon b. May 16, 1905
Glenn Cunningham—middle distances b. August 4, 1909
Forrest Towns—high hurdles b. February 6, 1914
Archie Williams—long sprints b. May 1, 1915
John Woodruff—middle distances runner b. July 5, 1915
Payton Jordan, coach b. March 19, 1917
Berny Wagner, coach b. 1924
Bob Richards—pole vault b. February 20, 1926
Bob Mathias—decathlon b. November 19, 1930
Wes Santee—mile runner b. March 25, 1932
Lee Calhoun—high hurdles b. February 23, 1933
Al Oerter—discus b. September 19, 1936
Bill Toomey—decathlon b. January 10, 1939
Dick Fosbury—high jump b. March 6, 1947
Bruce Jenner—decathlon b. Oct. 28, 1949
Craig Virgin—cross country b. August 2, 1955

Appendix B: Descriptions of the Olympic Events

100 Meter Dash

Considered the premiere event of outdoor track, the 100-meter dash requires speed and strategy. Originally, runners started from a standing position and sprinted the distance to the finish line. But in 1887, Charles Sherrill dug small foot holes in the track and started his run from a crouching position. The "crouch" is still used by runners today.

Since 1937, runners have used starting blocks, and more recently, cinder and dirt tracks have given way to tracks composed of synthetic material, to permit running in all kinds of weather.

Originally, the race was 100 yards or 91.44 meters, but as racing became international, the race was standardized to 100 meters. Only races that are electronically recorded are accepted by the IAAF for world record consideration. Timing devices can measure times to one-hundredth of a second, and high speed photography can picture a win in one-thousandth of a second.

Ratification of records also requires a wind gauge reading, with a tailwind of no more than 2 meters/second permitted.

200 Meter Race

200-meter sprinters must possess all the speed required for the 100-meter dash, as well as a strategy to deal with the added challenge of a curved track. Although 200-meter competitions were held on straight tracks in the U.S. until 1958, the race has been run with a full bend on a 400-meter track at the Olympics, since it was introduced in 1900. Beginning in the 1960s two sets of records have been kept for these races. Speeds range from three-tenths to four-tenths of a second faster on a straight racing surface, as the runner is held back by centrifugal force on a curved track.

400 Meter Race/440 Yards

The quarter mile race (440 yards) was originally intended to be a test of a runner's endurance. Currently, the 400-meter race is run in lanes, like a sprint, with two to seven competitors. Because of the added length (compared to the 100- and 200-meter races), the 400 meters is a test both of speed and stamina. It also tests the athlete's determination to overcome physiological limitations. This race is sometimes dubbed "the man killer" because muscles are deprived of oxygen after about 30–35 seconds at sprint speed, causing severe pain.

800 Meter Race

This race, which requires both speed and endurance, has been a part of competitive sport since 1830. The original strategy of the race was to use speed to gain an initial lead, but in the 1930s it was discovered that faster times could be achieved by running evenly-paced laps. The introduction of interval training (fast repetitions with short recoveries) by German coaches in the late 30s further decreased the record times of this race. After 1959, the 800-meter competition was run in lanes for the first 300 meters, to avoid the jostling that occurred at the start of these races. In some of the current competitions, the length of the starting lane has been reduced to 100 meters.

1500 Meter Race

The 1500-meter race requires athletes to have speed, strength, and a strategy that allows them to maximize their individual running styles. The 1500-meter race originated on the 500-meter European tracks, and has been a part of the modern Olympic competitions since they were reborn in 1896.

Many 1500-meter racers also competed in the 5000-meter race early on. Paavo Nurmi of Finland was the first Olympic champion in both events, which he won in less than an hour in 1924, at the Paris games.

Long, cross-country training runs, twice a day, were introduced by Gosta Olander and brought the world's record down to 3:43. Intensive, speed-oriented interval training came into popular use in the 1960s, with the accomplishments of Jim Ryun of the U.S. Then, Filbert Bayi of Tanzania broke the world record in 1974 with a run of 3:32.2. Today, this distance run is dominated by athletes from North Africa, who follow rigorous training schedules.

110 Meter Hurdles

The 110-meter hurdle races are not a running and jumping event, but rather a sprint over a series of ten barriers—42 inches high—placed ten yards apart. Hurdlers stretch their stride patterns to take only three steps between the hurdles.

The modern running of 110-meter hurdles began in England about 175 years ago, as an obstacle course variation of the 100-yard dash. The hurdles competition became a 120-yard race in 1864. It featured wooden barriers placed 15 yards from both the start and finish lines, and eight additional hurdles spaced 10 yards apart in the lanes. In 1888, 28 centimeters were added to the distance, to create the 110-meter hurdles event.

At first, hurdlers tucked their legs under their bodies to clear the barriers, in a technique known as "bundling." Greater speed was achieved by using a stride to clear the hurdle, followed by three steps between barriers. Originally, the hurdles were heavy, fixed wooden obstacles. But by the time of the 1896 Games, the hurdles were more lightweight, and configured with an inverted T-base that allowed them to be knocked over.

The L-shaped hurdle with an eight pound counterbalance was introduced in 1935. This allowed the barrier to fall over easily, and diminished the risk of runner injury. Until 1935, athletes were disqualified if they knocked over more than three hurdles, and denied any records earned if they knocked over a single barrier.

The Decathlon

The decathlon involves the all-around ability of an athlete in tests of speed, strength and endurance. The competition takes place over a two-day period in ten different track and field events. The **100-meter race**, to test leg speed, is the first event on the first day. This event is followed in order by the **long jump**, to test leaping ability, the **shot put** (arm strength), the **high jump** (leaping ability) and **400-meter race** (speed and stamina).

The second day's events begin with the **110-meter hurdles**, which demonstrate speed and agility, the **discus throw** (strength and throwing ability), the **pole vault** (strength and agility), the **javelin throw** (throwing ability) and the **1500-meter race**, the final test of endurance.

Although there are some subjective judgments made in the competition, an international scoring table is provided to evaluate and award points for each performance. The athlete who has earned the most points at the end of the ten events is the winner.

Because few athletes can aspire to the highest performance in all of the events, they make concessions in their preparation, to maximize their total score. By fine-tuning their best events and working on the ones in which they are less proficient, they try to add as many points as possible.

The key element in the decathlon is endurance—athletes must perform at their best over a two day period, in events that often require 8–10 hours of intense competition each day. There are also mental factors that affect performance. An athlete cannot lose focus if he does less than his best in a single event. Successful decathletes pick themselves up, refocus, and move to the next competition. Disappointment in a performance and fear of failure are the decathlete's most formidable opponents.

Decathletes tend not to compete against each other as much as against the scoring table and their own fatigue. Breaks between events offer time for competitors to help and encourage each other toward their personal best.

Organizers of the 1912 Stockholm Olympics planned the first decathlon of the modern day Olympics. The term "decathlon" was first used in the Scandinavian countries and derives from the Greek words "deka" meaning ten, and "athlos," a contest. In the early part of the 20th century decathlons were staged in both Sweden and Denmark, with differing scoring tables and order of competitive events.

The first modern decathlon was held in Sweden in 1911, as practice for the upcoming Games in Stockholm the following year. The events and their sequence were the same as those followed today. Jim Thorpe won the first gold medals in the modern decathlon and pentathlon, and no one surpassed his performances for fifteen years.

A year after his unprecedented victories in Stockholm, Thorpe's medals were taken away, for a perceived infraction of his amateur status. He went on to play baseball and football, and was the first president of the NFL. Thorpe died penniless, but in 1982, his record was re-entered in the Olympic books and facsimile medals were presented to his family.

The Discus Throw

The sport of discus throwing first appeared in the ancient Olympic Games in 708 BC, and was revived for the Games in Athens in 1896. The discus throw is a well-described event in Greek history, where it is documented that the discs were made first of stone and then bronze. They weighed 2–6 kilograms and were 21–34 centimeters in diameter. The discus was thrown from a pedestal, which measured 60 by 70 centimeters. During that same time period, athletes in Sweden threw the discus from a 2.5-meter square.

With the revival of the Olympic Games, the throwing area, style of throw, weight and size of the discus became standardized. The disc was standardized for weight and size in 1907 at 22 centimeters in diameter and 2 kilograms in weight. The U.S. used a seven foot (2.13-meter) diameter circle in 1897, which was increased to 2.50 meters (8.2 feet) in 1908. Styles of throwing changed during the early part of the 20th century, moving from the static throw of 1900 to the Nordic swinging throw, to the turn and skip release throw introduced by Clarence Houser of the U.S.A in 1926.

Contests using two hands were held until 1920, when the current one-hand throw became the norm. Introduction of the concrete throwing platform in 1954 helped athletes attain greater rotation speed.

Distance Running

Distance running was introduced to the U.S. in 1880, when the Amateur Athletic Federation began holding competitions. The National Cross Country Association held its first competition in 1887. Competition at the collegiate level soon followed, and the Intercollegiate Cross-Country Association was organized in 1898. The NCAA assumed jurisdiction over the national championship event in 1938, and the IAAF assumed international control in 1962.

Long-distance racing demands mental determination and aerobic conditioning to develop the necessary stamina.

Cross-country events are those which are run over open country on trails, as opposed to track and field events, which compete on roads or tracks. Although there is no standardized distance, the IAAF sets a 12,000-meter minimum, or about 7½ miles.

Long distance running includes the five kilometer, ten kilometer, half marathon and marathon events. Statisticians, who compare the performances of world record holders in distance running, estimate that athletes reach their peak in the five kilometer race at age 27, the ten kilometer at 29, and the marathon at ages 31 to 37.

Most coaches of distance runners agree that training must vary with the individual athlete. Although there is an emphasis on the development of strength and endurance for this competition, each runner brings different strengths and weaknesses to the race, which must be addressed individually.

High Jump

High jumping was introduced into the Western world by the Celts, and the first competitions were held in England in 1840. In 1865, rules were established that allowed three jumps at each height, and jumpers could not take off with both feet (a rule that still holds in competitions today). Until 1936, the crossbar had to be jumped feet first.

Throughout the years, a variety of jumping styles were introduced— the Scissors, the Eastern Cut-off, the Western Roll, the Straddle, and in 1968, the Fosbury Flop, which has been used by most jumpers since the late 70s—from high school competitors to Olympians.

The high jump can be broken down into three phases: run-up, takeoff and bar clearance. In the Fosbury-flop, the athlete twists in the take-off, producing a near 180 degree rotation. The bar is cleared by a somersault position that arches the back, lowers the head and lifts the knees. In a correct fall, the jumper lands on his back and shoulders on a foam mattress. (Fosbury used a shavings pit originally.)

Fosbury's coach, **Berny Wagner**, once hypothesized that Fosbury's approach to the high jump paralleled the efforts of gymnasts, who achieve optimal height at the end of a routine by turning around and jumping backwards.

Javelin Throw

In this event, the athlete grasps a metal and fiberglass spear, runs up a rubberized surface area to a painted line, and releases the javelin. It must hit the ground tip first, within a sector 29 degrees wide, to be considered a legal throw. The javelin itself is approximately 8½ feet long and weighs just under two pounds.

Although the javelin is a throwing event, performance is enhanced by the speed of the run-up, which generates the forward velocity of the spear. A form of javelin throwing was included in the ancient Olympics, but the goal was not distance of throw, but rather accuracy in hitting a target.

Long Jump

In this event, the athlete races down a runway to a white line and leaps into a sand pit. The distance of the jump is measured from the furthest back point in the sand where the athlete lands. A foul occurs if the athlete's foot crosses the white line before a jump, and no score is given. Long jumpers must focus on their steps, speed of approach, the height of the jump, distance and landing. Athletes practice their approach, running backwards on the runway, to determine the exact number of steps needed to reach the white line.

Speed is important, because it gives momentum to the jump. Athletes also try to gain as much height as possible before they land. Many go up on one foot and bend the other toward the chest; others reach for their toes with their hands. A good landing is critical; leaning back to brace a fall could take inches or even feet off the distance.

The Mile

Many middle distance runners also run the mile, which is 1609.32 meters. The mile run requires endurance, speed, and the ability to use strategy under pressure. Runners need to reach the halfway point in the race at a good pace, and still feel in control. Mile runners often develop this skill by running at varying paces, with repetitions of shorter distances, such as 400 or 800 meters.

Milers prepare for competition in many different ways. Some run hard for short distances, while others include longer distance runs in their schedules. Some of the more successful runners say that they concentrate on winning, have a pacing strategy, maintain focus, and stay as calm as possible before the race, to preserve the adrenalin-release energy needed for the race.

Other competitive milers take their own bedding when they stay in hotels before a race. They follow a familiar routine, take a relaxing solitary walk or go over their racing strategy, until their focus on winning can resist last minute distractions at the track.

Pole Vault

History tells us that the sport of pole vaulting was known to the ancient Greeks. In Crete, athletes used long poles to vault over bulls. Celts, in ancient Britain, vaulted for length. In the 18th century, pole vaulting emerged in Germany, as a competition in vertical gymnastics.

Poles used in vaulting were usually made of ash, and athletes climbed them as they jumped. Americans were the first vaulters to disallow the movement of hands along the pole. The running pole leap began to appear in competitions in the middle of the 19th century.

Pole vaulting was part of the first modern Olympics at the 1896 Games. The competition was won by William Welles Hoyt, an American who vaulted ten feet, ten inches, to achieve the gold. At the turn of the century, vaulters began to reverse their legs upwards to clear the bar, with their stomach facing down.

The introduction of lighter and stronger materials for the pole raised vaulting performance. Lightweight bamboo poles were introduced in 1900, followed by aluminum, steel and fiberglass. The fiberglass pole was first used in the U.S. in 1956, and the first world record using this material was set in 1961.

The receiving box for the pole was not part of the sport until 1942. Landing mattresses were introduced in the 1950s, which improved safety for vaulters.

Shot Put

Although the shot put competition is classified as a "throwing" event, the shot put is not thrown, but pushed or "putted." The shot putter stands within a concrete throwing circle seven feet wide, and "puts" a 16 pound iron ball to land within a sector of 40 degrees.

To prepare for the throw, the athlete faces the back of the circle, curls his fingers around the shot and rests his hand against his shoulder, with the shot under his chin. He bounds or hops across the circle in a half crouch, turns and builds up speed. When he reaches the far end of the circle he faces forward, straightens and pushes the shot, by uncoiling his arm and body.

A throw is disqualified if the shot putter steps out of the throwing circle, or if the shot lands outside the 40 degree sector lines. The put can be made from the shoulder with one arm only, and must not be brought behind the shoulder.

To qualify for competition, each athlete makes three throws, and the seven best are allowed an additional three throws. Athletes are ranked according to the distance of their longest throw. To compete in the shot put requires speed, and great strength in both arms and legs. Shot putters typically train with weights, to develop the power necessary to "push" the iron ball in competition.

The shot put may have begun with rock throwing competitions by soldiers in ancient Greece. King Henry VIII held court competitions for weight throwing, and in the 1600s, cannonball throwing competitions were a favorite sport for English soldiers.

In 1860, weights were thrown from squares, seven feet on each side, but this configuration was changed in 1906 to the seven foot diameter circle, and the shot weight was established at 16 pounds. At that time, it was also determined that throwers cannot bend their arms (to reduce injury) and must hold the shot in the crook of their neck before it is released.

The U.S. has originated several new techniques in the shot put, beginning in 1876, with the sidestep action inside the throwing circle. In 1951, Parry O'Brien developed a style in which he faced the back of the circle, and then rotated 180 degrees before moving across the circle to make his final release.

The rotational technique was introduced in 1976 by Aleksandr Baryshnikov of the Soviet Union, a style similar to that used by discus throwers.

Appendix C:
Historical List of the
Modern Olympic Games

1896–Games of the I Olympiad, Athens, Greece
1900–Games of the II Olympiad, Paris, France
1904–Games of the III Olympiad, St. Louis, United States
1906–Intercalated Games, Athens, Greece
1908–Games of the IV Olympiad, London, Great Britain
1912–Games of the V Olympiad, Stockholm, Sweden
1916–Games of the VI Olympiad, Berlin, Germany
Cancelled because of World War I
1920–Games of the VII Olympiad, Antwerp, Belgium
1924–Games of the VIII Olympiad, Paris, France
1928–Games of the IX Olympiad, Amsterdam, Netherlands
1932–Games of the X Olympiad, Los Angeles, United States
1936–Games of the XI Olympiad, Berlin, Germany
1940–Games of the XII Olympiad, Helsinki Finland.
Cancelled because of World War II
1944–Games of the XIII Olympiad, London, Great Britain
Cancelled because of World War II
1948–Games of the XIV Olympiad, London, Great Britain
1952–Games of the XV Olympiad, Helsinki, Finland
1956–Games of the XVI Olympiad, Melbourne, Australia
1960–Games of the XVII Olympiad, Rome, Italy
1964–Games of XVIII Olympiad, Tokyo, Japan

1968–Games of the XIX Olympiad, Mexico City, Mexico
1972–Games of the XX Olympiad, Munich, West Germany
1976–Games of the XXI Olympiad, Montréal, Canada
1980–Games of the XXII Olympiad, Moscow, Soviet Union
1984–Games of the XXIII Olympiad, Los Angeles, United States
1988–Games of the XXIV Olympiad, Seoul, South Korea
1992–Games of the XXV Olympiad, Barcelona, Spain
1996–Games of the XXVI Olympiad, Atlanta, United States
2000–Games of the XXVII Olympiad, Sydney, Australia
2004–Games of the XXVIII Olympiad, Athens, Greece
2008–Games of the XXIX Olympiad, Beijing, China

Index

*Numbers in **bold** indicate pages with photographs.*